Blerim Burjani

Possible or Impossible Final Agreement Between Kosovo and Serbia

Blerim Burjani

Possible or Impossible Final Agreement Between Kosovo and Serbia

Normalization Relation

Dictus Publishing

Imprint
Any brand names and product names mentioned in this book are subject to trademark, brand or patent protection and are trademarks or registered trademarks of their respective holders. The use of brand names, product names, common names, trade names, product descriptions etc. even without a particular marking in this work is in no way to be construed to mean that such names may be regarded as unrestricted in respect of trademark and brand protection legislation and could thus be used by anyone.

Cover image: www.ingimage.com

Publisher:
Dictus Publishing
is a trademark of
Dodo Books Indian Ocean Ltd. and OmniScriptum S.R.L publishing group

120 High Road, East Finchley, London, N2 9ED, United Kingdom
Str. Armeneasca 28/1, office 1, Chisinau MD-2012, Republic of Moldova, Europe
Printed at: see last page
ISBN: 978-613-7-35702-6

INSTITUTI I KOSOVES PER POLITIKA ZHVILLIMORE (IKPZH)

BLERIM BURJANI

Possible or impossible final agreement for normalization of Kosovo-Serbia relations

Email:instiuti_politik@yahoo.com

Number of telephone +383/44502546

burjani@yahoo.com

PRISTINA , 2018

ASM - Association of Serbian Municipalities

PDK-Democratic Parties of Kosovo

LDK-Democratic Ligue   of Kosovo

LVV –Movement for Self Determination

List of Serb- Serbian List

Entry.. 5

Kosovo and North part   of country.. 8

Serbia made obstacles Kosovo.. 11

The EU is formulating political positions for states.................... 13

EU And Final Talks... 21

Opposition political parties in Kosovo...................................25

What does it mean for the state of Kosovo............................. 34

Kosovo and Serbs minority.. 41

Conflicts and panic - Serbian politicians more trust SNS Vučićic than the current prime minister..43

Opposition divided in Kosovo 45

Third Strategy of Serbia 51

Kosovo strategy and options.. 52

The international community measured against Serbia and the issue of the recognition of the state of Kosovo 55

Constitutional changes at the doorstep................................. 57

The EU calls for reforms to take place in Kosovo 59

Free interpretation for: "Agreement of the Association of Serbian Municipalities".. 66

Even Albania against the exchange of territories Kosovo-Serbia 70

Failure to reach a political consensus in Kosovo 71

BLERIM BURJANI – statements 74

The new government after the elections 76

Lunaqek in CEC 79

Serbian List 80

Special Court 82

The Kosovo-Serbia dialogue with a clear goal......................... 87

Perfidy of Vučić's politics towards Macedonia 91

Conclusions... 97

Entry

Chronology of development of political inquiries under technical dialogue umbrella Kosovo –Serbia. It was interesting how the technical level dialogue become political talks that means- took another dimension of talks between two countries, which took place political aspect without clearly understanding what are the interests of the Kosovo in this process, and the other side of the conviction to enter into these talks to bring Serbia to the EU and bring political "peace" , between countries with no doubts in the end of dialogue but "no guaranties with happy".

 But until now there are a lot confusion in direction what is the purpose of interests of Kosovo expectations of achieving stability in western Balkan? Or what else interest has Kosovo's state according to easily EU integration ? Even the public opinion in Kosovo for these talks Kosovo-Serbia, is full of debates and many suspicions and without any doubt, these talks were full of an-normal political confidences with certain aims, and the idea was to avoid public opinion and the noise that it could be done during this dialog. The normal purpose was to hide the agenda and the exact address of problems, without problem definitions and solutions should be made in this negotiation? An argument was interesting and odd when the UN had request to the Belgrade to enter into negotiations with Pristina only for technical purpose and to find solution based on needs of two country, despite all that it was known that these the talks have nothing to do with the so-called technical normalized process, but talks which had been interpreted as the normalization of relations that ultimately were disowned by Cooper himself and the international factor. This was clear, even then when it had accepted Serbia to talk with the State of Kosovo to realize its own interests during this dialog according the same strategy to divide Kosovo in ethnic life. International strategy could have been that there would be "partial" and technical talks as much as two parts needed. There some doubts that the Serbia have agreed to negotiate under some conditions and promises that they could have earlier from international factor, earlier or later they will come out on surface maybe very soon. There was also dissatisfaction in Serbia over the talks begun at that time, but Tadic and Dacic did not have the courage to assure the Serbian public that these talks were not harmful so as the political agenda concerning agenda was prepared in Brussels. Tadic strengthened the support circle in the Assembly of Serbia. Tadic and other Serbian officials had also made promises to the citizens of northern Kosovo that they would not remain without support. Understandably the efforts to organize the illegal elections of Serbia in north part of state of Kosovo are possible and real during the all this period from 1999 until now. What is interest of Kosovo? Normalization relation with Serbia in Kosovo has begun to arrive the great political confusion, which it happened until now without political open explanations. The leaders in Kosovo are seeing that they have a functional logical flow once a footnote and then talk about the north of Kosovo state ?And what later to divide Kosovo by exchange ethnic territory three municipal of Kosovo in north to join Serbia and three Albanian municipalities in Serbia should join to Kosovo state? I have the impression that we are completely uninformed It is not known how long it will go and where is the end of these talks and which is final solution , it's going to be the full normalized relation with Serbia? Or its going to be limited normalized relation? At present there is no logical balance in dealing with problems. The game of international pragmatism and the confusion of politics in Kosovo is continuing to be expressed in unclear dimensions. Our policy should change as soon as possible the negotiating team should be establish. Thaci's political assistant - Edita Tahiri gives a clear signal that Thaci wants to remain outside the public opinion dialogue to keep position of the negotiator, and to have the greatest impact and the efficiency until the end of this dialogue. I think that waiving this non-tranparent should end here and a new negotiating team will have to be establish it have completely to change the negotiation approach in this new situation with a new team , more prepared and responsive negotiating team in front of the Kosovo Assembly. "We have a completely passive status in negotiation and without any document or the concept presentation on this dialogue, for what" Kosovo went into the talks"? Never been made public, as well   it was not clear who appointed her -Edita to be a chief negotiator of Kosovo and these talks, and sometimes even prime minister said that there was no other person who had defeated to accept this role from the ruling party, these are the dilemma that remained for all the time while hiding that there would be "technical" and "non-political talks was part of the alleged scenario for success after the talks". The team was without any ideas or models or scenario versions that it would have to orient the talks for the benefit of the state of Kosovo and this mysterious passive and non-productive approach dialogue which has brought bad political consequences and can bring even more unpleasant political situations in future. Cooper had done the agenda, and had done the job as well for what would be discussed? But not the Kosovar side which that had no ideas and rules or model scenarios where the beginning negotiation started with an-know the end. Politically it is costly without knowing how to propose many versions of solutions, or alternatives and how to maintain the state's interest. Serbian side part it is prepared much for proposing models, strengthens its position in dialogue and interests. This model of negotiation needs to be revised and it needs to be assembled for numerous models and versions by side of Kosovo team negotiation, normal during the talks must also have sustainability in the process and ability to withstand the pressures that may come from the mediator by respecting the position of good services, but Kosovo side also to demonstrate the interest of the state clearly and sometimes even so as to create a good credibility with the internal factor. Governance of state interest is particular importance to bring positivity to action. We hope that the situation will be better in the future, until now what we seen is not "look good". It would be good to develop unity strategy in Kosovo through parliamentary groups and to give them strategic importance to our state's interests. There is little hope that we can move faster to European integration because there are many things that need to be changed in the country. Should improve the function of state such as the prevention of corruption and stop much is possible bad indication in economy. The functioning of law and order much better ,to implement the justice reform, administration reform that can be fulfilled EU condition needed , that needs to be met in the first place. And normal north of the state need a solution which should be found, but the work was not doing well. It is now being sought for greater unity of position and opposition in Kosovo   and to find a functional model for working together for our country.

Serbia's attempt to organize Serbian elections in the north of the state of Kosovo since the 1999. Recently many Serbian officials has talking about Serbian elections in the north of Kosovo with bad organization and manipulation of election. If we analyze well there are many proposal pro and contra opinions of holding these elections in Kosovo, but never Kosovo institutions stopped these Serbian elections in north part of state of Kosovo , a part of the opinions in Serbia thinks that such elections should be held regardless of whether they will be void or without any legal effect, whereas there is such in Serbia that trumpeted the legitimacy of the elections. Major commercial or campaign declarations are being made in Serbia for the purpose of obtaining votes in Kosovo Serbs in north, even the young Serbs generations in Serbia there do not deal or is interested for Kosovo , but Serbia's official policy tends to propagate the old Serbian myths and this does not lead to any positiveness in relations with the state of Kosovo and generally normalization of relations between the two states. Perhaps more or less is to come to wonder when the EU thinks that Vucic party will bring some positive change in the wind of current European developments. This seems to be a rhetoric of words because Vucic and Dacic as politicians will not bring the European spirit of developments in Serbia or bring about so-called rational and modern "Serbian nationalism".

CHAPTER ONE

1.Kosovo and North part   of country

Since 1999, the Serb-inhabited north of Kosovo had been governed as *de facto* independent from the Albanian-dominated government in Pristina. It used Serbian national symbols and participated in Serbian national elections, which are boycotted the rest election organize from Kosovo institution ; and they boycotted all level Kosovo's state elections.

 The municipalities of Leposavić, Zvečan and Zubin Potok run by local Serbs, while the Mitrovica municipality separated from other part of Mitrovica which was unique before the war. Later in north was established two municipalities after the war the city has only one mayor population in north. Serbs were active participants in the Kosovo Elections in 2013.The Serbian was united into one territory self-called as the Union of Serbian Districts and this illegal "District Units of Kosovo" established in February 2008 by Serbian delegates meeting in Mitrovica, which has since served as North Kosovo's capital. The Union's President is Dragan Velić. This union is not recognized by the Republic of Kosovo, or by UNMIK and was abolished in 2013 as a result of the Brussels Agreement.

There is also a central governing body, the *Serbian National Council for Kosovo* (SNV). The President of the SNV in North Kosovo is Dr. Milan Ivanović, while the head of its Executive Council she was Rada Trajković. Local politics are dominated by the Serbian List for Kosovo. The Serbian List is led by Oliver Ivanović, an engineer from Mitrovica which was killed from Serbian illegal secret forces in north of Kosovo . The north of the state of Kosovo is inhabited by the Serbian minority, these municipalities are dominated by Kosovo Serb residents and differ from others, is bordered directly to central Serbia. This had alleviated its ability to govern itself almost completely independent of Kosovo institutions de facto separated by Kosovo authorities, Serb residents are directly in Belgrade's influence and pressure respected direct rules coming from of Belgrade, which they believe to be the authority "legal framework on Kosovo" as a whole.

North part of Kosovo

North Kosovo is out of control of state institutions of Kosovo, the north is a criminal area involved in smuggling cigarettes, gas, drugs and prostitution, until now everything has happened in this part and no one has any responsibility either from Kosovo or from Serbia. Serbian authorities hold full responsibility for criminality in the north. Crime criminals in Serbia find refuge in northern Kosovo. However, despite the fact that the region is close to Central Serbia, its location within Kosovo and based on the Kumanovo Treaty in 1999 means that only UNMIK officials have the freedom of movement in northern Kosovo, where they have sovereign status in that part of Kosovo, now this situation has changed the Kosovo police even the special one intervenes in the north in critical situations. Prior to the declaration of Kosovo's independence in 2008, it was speculated that Kosovo could be divided with the northern part of Kosovo while remaining part of Serbia's part. The complexity of the region has been on the Pristina-Belgrade 2011 agenda.

Actual situation

There are many remarks from Serbian residents minority in Kosovo on the influence and pressure which they have on Serbs in Kosovo by the state of Serbia, orienting them for voting in both Serbian national elections and general elections in Kosovo. The last time to Belgrade was have many remarks by local Serbs on Serbian government , they complain that they are wrongfully deceived to hear the Serbian party of having to vote in Kosovo. Serbian President Vucic seems to be the most influential man to local Kosovo Serbs. Kosovar Serbs complain that they do not have the freedom of opinion and free political action in Kosovo, they seek to orient their lives without the influence of Pristina and Belgrade, this is an important moment for local Serbs to live free and politically independent as residents of the state of Kosovo. Local Serbs have received two salaries and have not paid any electricity services and other services like property tax and other taxes almost 18 years , that means from 1999 . In January 2018, the Ombudsperson of Kosovo took the initiative that the debts of the Serbian minority for the current year do not pay the rest of the citizens of Kosovo and compensate the taxes paid for electricity spent in the north of the state of Kosovo, but Government of Kosovo State did not stopped this an logic situation. Serbia has often sought unofficially or autonomous for Serbs or their separation from Kosovo, a compromise was reached to establish a community of Serb municipalities in Brussels, while still today has a great deal of attention in this regard by a Kosovo legal expert and the Constitutional Court and the political parties for the creation of such an association, which does not allow the constitution of the state of Kosovo and is in contradiction with the law on local self-government. Kosovo is the most specific state in the building of local government through ethnic decentralization. In November 2012, Prime Minister of Kosovo Hashim Thaçi stated that autonomy for Northern Kosovo will never be granted, and the region will always remain a part of the Republic of Kosovo.

1.2.Serbia made obstacles Kosovo

Serbia had played obstructive roles to membership of Kosovo in international organizations and international regional ones as well , despite that it had secured the EU that will not stop Kosovo for membership in international organizations. Kosovo has a problem to become a member of UNSCO , but is recognize from 115 country member of UN and recognize by 23 state of EU including United Kingdom which is not more parte of EU. Kosovo is a member of 63 regional and international organizations and expressed interest in joining the Council of Europe and as well as EUROPOL. Serbia continues to hinder Kosovo's membership in the UN and hinder recognition for the state of Kosovo. Kosovo now is member of EUFA and FIFA.

1.3.Matter of cadastral documents and dialing code

A matter of cadastral documents to be returned from Serbia has been blocked for two years, without progress at all in meanwhile occurred many problems in some parts of State of   Kosovo without cadastral original documents , and another matter is that Kosovars are not yet using their own international dialing code despite the fact that two agreements were signed precisely about that. Many problems of implementation of agreements from Serbia side, until now yet is not possible Kosovo to use it's dialing code without any significant reasons given from Serbian authorities. Kosovo in the of all has a new code 383.

1.4.OSCE – Kosovo agreements for Serbian election in Kosovo

OSCE Agrees to Run Serbian Elections in Kosovo following the same pattern used for previous Serbian elections, the OSCE will handle the votes cast by Kosovo Serbs in the Serbian parliamentary elections. Serbian election in Kosovo held faced with many reaction from Kosovo opposition political party which they declare as against sovereignty of state of Kosovo.

1.5.All standing to stop Illegal Serb elections in the north of the state of Kosovo

It sounds funny when citizens hear such things as there will be no choice, of course many EU officials and the US say they should stop these elections to happened in they countries , while Serbian official politics had asked for opinion from UNMIK for election, of course all the answers look to be the same, there is no choice in the north organizing parallel life , but difficult to obey the current Serbian policy that in the north of the state of Kosovo cannot have such things, there are such excuses that the Ahtisaari plan recognizes duality, it is used by many politicians or Serbian state officials to say that the whole process can be developed on the principle of duality, such logic brings uncomfortable things to Pristina and the severity of the opposition to this process, while numerous voices have been gathered in the international community for the treatment of the north, the sui generic formula is the formula much Interestingly, all of these miracles that could happen in Kosovo but not in Bujanovac and Presevo and Medvedja in Serbia which lived ethnic Albanian municipalities, this also shows the balance of access to problems or persistent tendencies to speak for Kosovo's inner and sui generis formula in these reports. Political declarations in Kosovo do not cease to hold elections of Serbia in Kosovo, it is understood that everyone has declared that there will be no elections but there are statements where other forms are required to stop the elections in the north. The determination to stop illegal elections in the north by Serbia in the state of Kosovo requires measures and procedures. The determination is protected by decisive but not declarative and moral decisions for the need to take adequate measures to stop such illegal Serb elections that are in opposition to Kosovo's state interests. Measures and procedures imply an operational order of action and other things, and all of this requires an operational plan for the Ministry of Internal Affairs of the Republic of Kosovo, this is easy to do but a will is required political and application procedures that will not allow them to be held. Let's look at how the role of institutions in this subject will be energetic.

1.6. The EU is formulating political positions for states

It is a great political moments and time that Kosovo's state authority and Kosovo's foreign policy takes very seriously the political theme of the north country , to integrate it in Kosovo institution north and seek in an international guarantee that Serbia will not win the candidate status for EU, if barricades and parallel institutions in the north do not cease. These developments are expected to take place soon , and that official Pristina through institutions is failing to find the right and understandable diplomatic and political pathway to deploy other relevant reports to the international community, where this community will oblige Serbia differently in changing its approach to the state of Kosovo. Kosovo's fully guided by the international community is perhaps the main guarantee that the West would have no contractual relations with Serbia unless Serbia did the right moves to surface the other political will vis-à-vis the state In this way, the region can not integrate into the EU without solving many problems and over all political issues. Cooper will soon meet the Serbian negotiator and will very briefly express his opinion on talks with Kosovo to find the model of Kosovo's participation in international forums. It is an immediate request that some things have to happen for a short time that will push Serbia to take "giant leaps" in relation to Kosovo to stabilize the European integration process of the region. In this regard, it is necessary to have some very important political segments in relation to Serbia in a short time. At least the moves forward the new politics directed and the Serbian state   guarantees   should   be   very   hopeful   as   follows:

1. Serbia to accept a model of Kosovo's representation in international forums;

2. Serbia should extinguish the parallel structures in the north of the state of Kosovo;

3. The northern part of the state of Kosovo in a short period of time should be included in the elections for local authorities where elections will be organized by the Central Election Commission of the Republic of Kosovo;

4. Immediate removal of barricades in the northern part of the Republic of Kosovo.

Serbia is reluctant to accept a model of Kosovo's state representation in international forums. There are some proposals on the table, some are strange if compared to international practices, and some are interesting to discuss. Normal to be discussed the variants that are most acceptable to Kosovo and do not cause degradation but express in a way the objective and regional reality created in the region. Serbia cannot be "divorced from 1244", which seems to be "eternal" this formula. While the EU insists on abandoning Serbia from this normal representation formula to accept it to be lifted. But Serbia has constitutional and legal problems under the authorities in Serbia to do so. Serbia does not have many options to choose, it is probably the last time to make clear moves on whether to win EU candidate status or be forced to deal with more types of international diplomacy and pressure. is going to have to offer a solution to this, since Serbia has trouble making proposals other than 1244, and this formula is more "greeted", and Western states want something else altogether, a qualitative change in this segment. While Kosovo and its foreign policy is probably not doing the best job of lobbying that it must do and has supported this work entirely in one dealing with Serbia. Therefore, there is no serious seriousness in this approach by local institutions. Serbia also has a task to distribute its parallel structures in the state of Kosovo, and it is not ready to do so because of the many promises made by Serbian leaders during the visits made to that part. Can Serbia do so before March this year? Elections in the northern part of Kosovo for local authorities to be organized by Kosovo's state institutions can only come if Serbia will make substantial changes in the relationship with Kosovo. On the contrary there is nothing of this topic.

Barricades are no longer in "fashion" this has been understood by authorities in Serbia, but should be guaranteed that they are removed and will no longer be placed on key roads that hinder the flow of goods and people in that part of the state of Kosovo. Barricades should be removed as soon as possible and discussions and games cannot be there. These are conditions that I can hardly fill in for a short time and that the likelihood of winning candidate status is minimal even though the EU has made knowing that there will be a will on this topic, but Serbia should expect to make substantial changes in relation to the state of Kosovo. The issue of Kosovo-Serbia talks calls Serbia's government a political context with many issues of normalization of relations with the neighboring state. These were labeled as technical for fear of governmental dialogue with Serbia with inadequate political terminology. In formal way now happened the changes there is not parallel Serbian structures , all Serbian institution was integrated in Kosovo state institutions , but now they asked to implement a agreement for establish Serbian Association of Municipalities. Serb minorities took part in two national and local election organized by Kosovo State Central Commission.

1.7. Special Force of Police (ROSU) of State of Kosovo - intervene in north it was a political game of Kosovo or what?

The north issue and the July 25 event of the KPS - the special unit "Rosu" intervene in the north because it is looked that Serbia and local Serb they start to become threating for integrity of Kosovo and their planes to change the status in north, in that part of the State of Kosovo can not be tolerated any more , radically altered the international politics towards the north of Kosovo and was considered an unbearable situation. Institution of Kosovo they will remember the murder of a Kosovo policeman from Serbian parallel structure, dancing in the barricades in the north and killers , and the game of the mouse and the cat one tried to break the barricades. While the Serbs built other barricades in the presence of KFOR, and northern Serb leaders were factored into Serbia. Local politics should work on building an all-inclusive platform for the north of Kosovo's state and regional and international developments. The issue of dialogue to normalize relations with Serbia, our side perhaps sees in reaching an understanding through the international community that Serbia renounces Kosovo territory, is interesting when Kosovo's official policy calls on Serbia to respect the territorial integrity of Kosovo, meanwhile, Serbia continues the old games that are sometimes modified and served as new ones in the political plane with unchanging goals towards Kosovo. There is also no change in the attitude of the Serbs to Kosovo. Numerous debates on our television almost every night, we hear the same things and from the same people, these people who speak do not have any influence in relation to Serbia and the north but simply speak discuss various things that are wandering around the northern problem and without any opportunity to change something. It is well known that Kosovo's policy towards the north is dependent on Western states and this is seen in all relations dealing with the topic of relations between Kosovo and Serbia. To change the situation and to normalize the divisions between Kosovo and Serbia, the international community must be completely energetic, while local politics has become the international community. Suffice it to mention the government's sterile statement when a man talks about the engagement of international security mechanisms in the north and gives invalid declarations and sometimes ordinary citizen of Kosovo gets the impression that Kosovo can move or change the situation in the north through local institutions. In fact, this issue is very clear that it depends entirely on the international community and the international security forces. Political sincerity is lacking, and it would be better to have less such statements and better to strengthen the Kosovo international diplomacy sector to provide as much information on the situation in the north as well as the barricade game that Serbia does and capacity building security and design of the general platform for the north. Normally to clarify our interest outside of Kosovo. The northern part of the state of Kosovo must be protected for the moment with effective diplomacy in cooperation with the international mechanisms and dialogue through normalization of relations with this neighboring state, but not through the relocation of the local institutions because the international mechanisms operating in Kosovo have spokesmen in defined level of relocation that are quite professional for this job. The dialogue on normalization of Serbian relations is also leading the US and the EU, which is very positive in drawing conclusions in this dialogue to resolve practical problems between the two states. Lion's words and mouse actions are a key segment of dialogues that are being made in Kosovo on the issue of the north of the state of Kosovo. Sometimes it is to be assumed that these people who are called politicians who are currently a profile do not have any specific or even specific weight to change the situation. Orientation of Kosovo's diplomacy to lobby and influence international mechanisms or international politics on the issue of the north is the greatest favor that can be made to our state. The whole situation there depends on the influence and action of the international community, there have been various and perhaps strangely different opinions and proposals, supposedly to help with the solution, is said in some variants when one cannot behave politically and there is no possibility and Professional favors to offer solutions find it difficult to deal with ideas for solutions. More attention should be given to the context of political action and international circumstances and the development of international law in current circumstances, more information can help to solve some open issues at this moment, but when the ambassadors of Kosovo are also analyzed, who are then likely to be doing well, being linked to electoral promises or people who do not know what to do, have arrived to become a deputy. In local political vocabulary dominate many things that are repeated repeatedly and have the same meaning nothing new can be found in debates calling the same people that it is better to issue a repeating tape than to call people who say nothing else. It's serious in the normal international politics in big states when politicians and state officials talk about a matter they do not deal with the same strip of television said many times. But this is the truth for such people we cannot expect anything more. Therefore, in the international community, they have lost their seriousness even waiting for translators in embassies to translate statements given by various officials to say that they are repeating politicians. The north of the state of Kosovo is expected to emerge on the negotiating table. The longstanding existence of the North's problem and the inability of the international community and our state to resolve that situation are pointing to or reflecting the acceptance of a long-term problem that refers to Kosovo, such as the north of the state to resolve once and for all and holding hope in the international community that one day the north of the state will be fully integrated. In international practice there are two situations referring to political reports, if for a long time or a long period of time there is no solution it like such is addressed with a certain normal solution avoiding security problems as few problems but with legal-political substitute. Other situations in international practice have been resolved with respect for law and order. For a long time, it has been unofficially spoken since 2000, not least in many formal and informal meetings and roundtables, the "north" issue of our state, for which there was never a "remedy" for the preservation and extension of control of territorial integrity of Kosovo. Communist regime has played the geographic and ethnic map of Albanians, so it is no surprise that in the northern part of the area, cases of confrontation even the then communist regime had left the problems or confusion long time from1956. Not by accident, they once knew that in the event of a problem in the future, the one who would be more powerful would occupy each other the designated territory and it was well known that this could be opened after a time or period, and as such, the Serbian communist regime had been convinced that it would leave the borders and the later expansion if other situations were to happen. Now, after all the developments, it is emerging that the path of "legal divorce" and the further fragmentation of solutions should be found. There were many analysts which express their opinions   that Ahtisaari's plan and Kosovo negotiating group did not negotiate with Serbia in Vienna, but only the international community has a negotiation, so Vienna's political picture appears in talks on technical issues in Brussels where the locals are asked only consenting to anything else or from the Kosovar side is required only the acceptance of the legal and political reality of the document. It is now clear that the international community through this plan aimed to solve the main problem but not to other ethnic problems.Interestingly in this document, it is never mentioned in the first for the ethnic majority that who constituted and had established abstract, not significant, demographic terminology, for which it could develop a policy of "securities" and international conventions to find a solution acceptable to the parties. Our prospect and joy for the independence of our country, which has suffered many times and with a hundred year old pain, came with the independence of Kosovo. But there seemed to be other important facts that were gathered during the talks in Vienna. There were formulas for solving the main part of the problem, but other facts are now emerging, so it can be interpreted or broken down in the political language because it is now out of public opinion that the issue of the north will come up with the solution model, at least the statements of international officials or some of them, in other words, will come out at the international round table, due to not changing the situation on the ground. This is normal for the state of Kosovo unacceptable. The events of 17 March 2004 were one of its two-way indicators.The majority of Albanians wanted the independence required for many years and that the Serb minority and Serbia seek other models of territorial extradition or seizure as far as possible of the territory of Kosovo through pervasive politics and diplomacy, is now asking a question that nothing is meaningful in the independent state of Kosovo and can also be discussed about the many footnote, but not even the Presevo valley. So does the international community really think that it was not entirely happy with the Vienna talks? This is a question that needs to be opened! Because the terrain and the political field events speak differently even after the independence of Kosovo, so a form of political and diplomatic mischief is required through the development of talks with the UN blessing under the

EU border, and without pompous meanings and media publicity and debates 'ardent', to find formulas for the guarantees of the Serbian minority and perhaps for the Serbian appetite and for the north of our state. It was not repeated occasionally repeated by Serbian officials that Serbia wants historic agreement with Kosovo, this was the backstage game diplomatic means to find the path of reconciliation through such variants that such so-called technical talks are emerging politically and are emerging as affecting the status and territorial integrity of the country through possible and further fragmentation of the territory and with the future proposal of models of strange international and unprecedented . The extremely poorly led politics has led to this, while the local state policy of the state of Kosovo was not oriented to other scenarios of preserving its integrity, Serbian politics had a direction of territorial fragmentation and Serbian reasoning for political and historical fabrications and in the end even mystical. The weak negotiating team and without the strategy bring compromise and overcompensation to state interests, while the international community in that world has followed in particular the Serbian reactions that were extremely contradictory. While our country is overwhelmed by political euphoria, the international side begins to think about other political models for the future. And this is what we see now is nothing wrong, and even more painful is the footnote to compromise on national interests in the north of the country that is naturally considered extremely painful where Kosovo as the most renowned state of the world is facing diminishing influence its own political in the region and the sharing of geo-political and geo-stray interests of the Western Balkans. The scenario is now clearer as it is expected that the elections in Serbia will be completed and the north will be negotiated, if everything goes according to the strategic interests of those who have further analyzed what should be done, so the international plan looks in a way preserves and favors Vucic in elections in Serbia - which is a partner of the international community. For Kosovo it is easier because they will listen normal the international community on any topic that can be opened to co-operate is the idea as it seems. It is not the case that Kosovo politician,   media avoidance, because it politically makes less use as a negotiator, are also the negotiating instructions of the negotiator to preserve the personal integrity of the negotiator so that it can be used in the future, that is very apparent. Kosovo's interests should be on the change of the chief negotiator and the recomposing of another politically non-politically normal, more professionally prepared delegation, and to find the model of political change , not to talk about and accept the game with the territorial integrity of Kosovo and the things that does not coincide with the national and state interest of the country. This ultimately leads us to understand that I still have problems with the proper preparation of the potential teams to enter into talks and lack the proper experience to deal with the existing problems and do not find good action models for outstanding issues until now. Local politics should have models of settlement of the situation there by establishing the rule of law and stopping barricades there as well as creating guarantees there that will have a free movement for all citizens and international organizations operating in Kosovo.

1.8. EU And Final Talks

The EU finally talk Serbia , cannot be given the status of candidate for EU Serbia due to not marking progress in relation to Kosovo an normalize relation between stats . Serbia still has territorial claims on Kosovo as EU policy is oriented towards creating a climate of good understanding and good neighborliness among the Western Balkan states, so Serbia is unlikely to meet such criteria because its policy towards its neighbors has never changed until now, this EU has understood, so while there is no progress in relation to its neighbors, it cannot gain other privileges from the EU. This time between the Serbian rows it was announced that it will not be tolerated its behavior in relation to Kosovo. The constant dilation of the situation in the north of the Republic of Kosovo caused by Serbia in agreements with local Serb leaders nothing good is not bringing. The constant strengthening of Serbia's policy toward the state of Kosovo is beginning to be very expensive, the more important it is to realize that the European and civilization platform is not met with the constant medieval wishes or appetites. But the Serbian people should be careful not to manipulate Kosovo Serbs with interests that have been lost most of the time but to work on European integration. The political scandal in Serbia is not good, tensions have begun to rise due to failure to accept candidacy her EU membership and resigned. There is not much left or either that is the end of Serbian or EU analysts or isolation, this is the new formula that can begin to be practiced by Western states no one in the EU wants new controversy and old problems, all EU states aspirations are the development of economic existence due to the many fluctuations in Europe's financial markets. Europe cannot deal with medieval appetites and myths and legends or archives, so the time is for a greater awareness of the political circles in Serbia. Neither does the EU want the game of conditionality because it is a democratic and structural organism for the good of all in Europe unless it is necessary, I will gradually come up with the constant "constipation" constraint that normal I will not like Serbs there. The prospect is the future of making compromises because of higher interests can be a political solution for Serbia. Withdrawal from Kosovo is the only door to smoothly run into the EU, recognition of Kosovo by Serbia it would be very welcome from the EU and for 22 EU countries that have recognized Kosovo so far. And five other EU states as soon as they do this better will be. Now the EU leaders have seen that they cannot expect for unjustifiable reasons to push the recognition of Kosovo by these five EU members. Pressures on these states will increase in future. It may be conditional and apparently the EU has no other choice than to persuade these states to recognize the state of Kosovo in addition to the insistence and pressure that these 5 EU states have to do have not yet recognized Kosovo in relation to EU funds. Serbia has until March to improve relations with Kosovo and to make substantial progress in implementing the agreements so far achieved. The most problematic issue for Serbia is the north of the state of Kosovo, the courage of some local Serb leaders in the north of the state of Kosovo likely to heavily dedicate Serbia to EU integration policies. There is not much time left, Serbia is or is in a great snare that has bruised itself. It is interesting that pseudo-patriotism in Serbia is still surviving, and this has other things that are affecting the investments of EU states in this state or the increase of support funds. There is time but Serbia does not have, so no myths should be built new absurd but to choose the path of becoming part of today's civilization.

Serbian President Vucic is in crisis, not many other letters to "play" and other constraints from the EU are expected to become likely, because the EU will review Serbian interest in relation to Kosovo and will evaluate negative again if it is there is positive movement.

1.9. North between solution and dilemmas

It seems to me now that the agenda for the three northern municipalities of our country will be discussed at least at completely different levels and quite seriously. As somebody is pointing to it, it is time to outline any reasonable and acceptable solutions. While we say that the plan of Ahtisaari is the only solution seems to have something in the midst of this plan which seems to have been written quite seriously but that implementation in this part of the state of Kosovo has been missing. Many ideas for a different alternative within this plan can be something becomes reality between the demands of Serbian citizens there and the Ahtisaari plan on the other. This can be done or until now it is somewhat said or drafted. We have heard that there will probably be talks about the north of our state and it seems that this agenda can be prepared for the summer and start in the fall until the end of the year to see concrete results. This can be of any real and objective reality. The fate of the settlement there will begin to be solved in September. But this is still unknown. If this plan starts to be public then the likelihood will be quite realistic that some of the various excerpts of this plan will be made known to the public during summer months. The middle settlement and through the completion of the Ahtisaari plan was part of the debate on several variants but this had resulted in Prishtina's suspicions that it did not but remains perhaps the best internal processing of the Ahtisaari plan. Diplomacy will comes intensifying and it seems that by September of the next year it will bring a result which will dominate the reason for the non-existence of the north problem. The north issue has become segment not useful and has exceeded the basis of interest in some international circles. They want to see solutions rather "than words", this seems to be coming true or becoming reality by the end of next year. Northern nodes think they need a solution that gives them greater confidence that nothing will ever happen with their interests created for a long period of time. The absence even a solution to the Ahtisaari plan even though it seems a little interesting because that plan had once been written by different international jurists, internal political mechanisms as the opposition and the opposition did not have the courage to really think of something like this. The government there is interest in the Ahtisaari plan being implemented throughout the Kosovo state and even in the north and that there will be no other plan, the opposition has not taken much with this issue, although it has often happened that the opposition and the position are fully supported in the Ahtisaari plan and did not have any other own ideas or any original domestic plan for solving, and so the issue is dragging on for many reasons: the lack of courage in approach, dilemma, Ahtisaari's plan as the only solution remained and remain the only political thesis of local institutions. While it is said that international circles have been working on this topic in the north and the underlying document a few short points will be sent to the Kosovo institutions and they are expected to accept in a way such a short draft with some basic theses on the approach and then the variations on how to move on. Western States have understood they expect the elections in Serbia to end so that coming to the negotiating table of any elaborate plan that does not go beyond Ahtisaari's borders will be acceptable to Kosovo as long as Serbia needs to enjoy the goblets it wants they are offered to Serbs in the north, this is the best and easiest variance for Pristina as Serbia wants to be part of a solution to the north? The international community considers the position of Kosovo institutions as very reasonable and for this received positive grades, the last actions of Kosovo's institutions were relaxation and suppleness the situation in the north and in Serbia, because the Serbian political scene had got the political stalemate that they could not organize elections in the north, so Pristina compromise enabled them to overcome any possible jargon within Serb politicians, and this became a reality, Serbia's national and presidential elections were organized in the north, while the local ones were banned by agreement with Belgrade that they would not be held at that level, and that's what it likes politicians of all currents in Serbia because the principle of Serbian citizens in the north is legalized they are given double the vote or declaration of their political will, as long as they are not at all represented in Serbia and have no political influence in Serbia. But it is understood that the hands of Serbian Serb politicians are mixed in the north the state of Kosovo does not deny it through the numerous statements that become political in Serbia. Serbs citizens seem confused they hear but fear what will happen to them if the confusing currents are developing the political ones around them while some Serbian politicians who have become famous with the north thanks to the north issue have survived in Serbian politics, within the Serbian state is seen that they do not want a quick settlement of the north because they will remain without any significance in Serbia here are Vucic - that means they will lose their influence in Serbia man no longer will they can have important political positions and tell fairy tales in Serbia for Kosovo Serbs. It looks worrisome for those people who have capital in the north and depend on many businesses. However, we expect to see the introduction of a plan that may be perhaps the only solution for the north, namely Ahtisaari's plan and sketches with a short concept in the form of theses without any media propaganda but silent may be the solution of the north.North complicated issues and possible scenarios for solutions. Keeping the extraordinary session of the Kosovo Parliament for the north issue was quite interesting, of course, the position indicated "willingness and not willingness" to intervene, and thus interfering with one another to establish order and law in the north.

2. Opposition political parties in Kosovo : Red Borders - The opposition played the role of bravery? How well has the opposition in these cases? Especially in Kosovo, where it is objectively seen without the political and juridical power of the institutions and to make a decision. It is seen from this prism that hesitation and how to do with the north, or better with the expectation and the international community, assist them and find solutions. The parties in the coalition led by the executive indicated that this work is difficult and complicated because of the international community, especially KFOR and EULEX, because it is clear that it is not easy to find any solution or cannot intervene in the north without international consent. Until the opposition says it is easy to do it? While the EU has refused any interference in the north, it is interesting that "Normally you cannot expect the EU to say" intervene in the north "because consequences and other complications that may arise from the intervention process. It has impressed the various comments in the eve of the meeting of the Assembly of Kosovo - it was quite meaningful and very precise the words "difficult for solicitors" to come to a solution, normal state action is characterized with not many words with a clear analysis and undertaking of adequate measures to bring order and law to it part of the state of Kosovo. With words and discussions and debates on this topic is not resolved but with the undertaking of adequate measures and cooperation with the international community. It is expected in international co-ordination if there is already the international community interest to have any internal solution. The inter-ministerial interlocutors should be placed on the negotiating table in several versions:

2.1.Scenarios for the north

-Including internal dialogue with the citizens of the north in assisting the international factor in cooperation with the institutions of the state of Kosovo, this may be the first version of the beginning of the solution of the northern problem, which it considers should be put as an option first, in order to leave another variant in turn - the only inter-community interviews with the citizens there to find a solution and leave time to dialogue without intervention of the party of Kosovo and Serbia, third version joint tripartite Kosovo talks, inter-communal community and Serbia - this version is currently acceptable to the international community, unless there is any result to test the co-ordination of the international community and international security institutions to bring order and law there. The fourth version of the intervention seems to be complicated and this is being seen q gold does not depend solely on the institutions of the state of Kosovo but it all depends on the inter-communist community. From this analysis are seen the possible scenarios of solving the problem of the north. There seems first important dialogue with the international community for the northern part of the state of Kosovo, so a very intensive and serious dialogue where the modality of how to establish order and law should be considered. There is a need to use the scenarios, even though we lose quite a lot of time, perhaps we should consider the fact that even when critical moment of the developments in the north is being started work with potential scenarios. In International Practices it is verified that scenarios have the goals in each mode of action from the aspect of crisis resolution such scenarios have to be elaborated one by one to come to certain conclusions, this is because of the creation of the maturity process until the final drafting of the solution. Very few of us have worked on these scenarios, these scenarios can be processed by various security and rule-of-law experts and politicians who only support the option of experts, so it has happened in many countries that scenarios have made up the main role of the solutions. Only after the expansion of territorial integrity should the dialogue be opened for the organization of elections by the Kosovo institutions there and the other operational plan for the establishment of law and order institutions, but good will can be achieved, but of course there is a need for understanding and co-ordination activities with the international community. Delay ..., delay the beginning of the process of implementing the agreement. Once a problem as an agreement has been reached, the experience with Serbia does not surprise us differently for good, now a normal problem of the implementation of the agreement. It is understood that all have problem for implementation , if the agreement is reached, then a mechanism for implementation everyone knew in Brussels, and especially our delegation that Serbia has hardly been told by the agreement, and then it continues in other games, the ball goes to the Serbs of the north now, who are keen to continue with games of Similarly, the referendum issue is meaningless, or the northern Serbs play in the factoring paper beyond the agreement, as if they have made a normal strategy if the agreement is reached, then "B" does not implement it, but not with the northern Serbs in game. This significantly complicates the entire precession and returns it to the initial stage. Or is there any attempt to ask for a revision of this agreement by the parties that have linked it: under the slogan that local Serbs disagree, now Serbia is in a better position, it is enough to formally say yes also the agreement implementation plan and stop to cease until they do the "northern Serbs" game. It was very well known that they would resist, the problem was the proper implementation of the agreement, if they say yes the agreement between the Serbs of the north is known that they say no agreement.

2.2. Who will be responsible for these games of northern Serbs

Then whoever sustains the consequences of responsibility, there is no one except the northern Serbs, they will be the main bearer of responsibility in delaying the start of implementation. The Bush should think differently in this process, must find ways to implement the detailed plan for the implementation of the agreement otherwise, the agreement remains in the drawers of the parties. The mechanism was missing even earlier if the northern Serbs did not cooperate to implement the agreement. The issue of creating a mechanism for implementation - and I said much earlier, that we should think otherwise, Brussels's struggle is bad. It is not interest to fail the agreement, so they should probably take the United States together with the main role provided the implementation of the agreement. I do not see any positive movement I have seen before of the local Serbs who were still courageous and inspired by Serbian mythological nationalism, that those where they are supposed to be "the state", so these fairy tales are still in the north.

2.2. Serbia gives time to the north for the implementation of the plan agreements Certainly, the Serbian side will delay accepting the plan for implementing the agreement, while northern Serbs still earn time for nationalist moves and gain time to think about their destructiveness in this process, so it is not easy for Dacic and others who said yes to the agreement, they are changing the political rhetoric and are pointing to their word: they are for national interests but the west is not allowed and listened to increase their borders in the Balkans. These things and political rhetoric , are evidence before the West that the current government is not democratic but wants EU integration, so they want Serbian leaders to say more symbolic and dialogue and monotheism in Serbia to European states that they are to support Serbia's integration policy. now again three rounds of negotiations for approval of the plan to implement the agreement, that is In just a couple of months they will deal with the pre-implementation phase. Trusting Serbs is always difficult, but they do not have much choice, they should give their consent to the agreement.

2.3. Cooper should find a "medium" solution of Kosovo's representation in regional relations and beyond

Winter fever that has overtaken Kosovo, developments in the north of the state of Kosovo and Cooper talks to find a solution to Kosovo's representation model in regional and wider conferences are topics that have been sparked during this period with fever and congestion village bores and family tragedies at this time. They are also developments that characterize this 10-day time period. Cooper's diplomacy in Pristina and the attempt to create an international Kosovo representative report at regional and wider meetings are EU efforts to find the most acceptable model for Pristina and Belgrade was not good and sufficient. This time it is quite difficult to find a way out, because there are not many options proposed at the negotiating table negotiated by Cuper .Problems are evident and almost in an unresolved format due to perhaps poor proponent diplomacy. The parties insist on interests that are of significant significance, while the third party in this case is Cuper does not have any meaningful proposing pattern. Some international circles suggest that it can be a model of representation only with the term: Kosovo, and some other alternatives such as the footnote and the opinion of the ICJ or Resolution 1244. The latter considers it to be unacceptable and does not lead to a rolling back of dialogue and does not contribute more in solution.

2.3. While labels R. Kosovo without the use of "footnotes", it may be probably an efficient variant.It is difficult to imagine that our country remains in the "footnote", which loses real and objective meaning in international law or other similar practices. One issue is known that it is important for Serbia to at least agree with a variant and it has agreed, but the issue lies to Kosovo that cannot accept such legal artificial such is footnote and Resolution of UN 1244 which is not more important for political development in real political life in Kosovo and in international policy. That is, it is not acceptable to mention in 1244 current relations and new objective reality in these international reports. It is not good for anyone to learn for the new state of Kosovo for the rejection of such denigrating formulas. This implies that international diplomacy is in crisis because of its unwillingness to propose many variants that the states will accept. This suggests that much work remains to be done to find effective solutions to Kosovo's handling of international relations. Valid options seem to be absent, there is no adequate formula that Kuper would propose would be the end of the Serbian blockade at the same time. The other issue remains the north of the state of Kosovo - the barricades and threats of the Serbian minority and the illegal referendum. Serbian threat policy continues to be a strong political and diplomatic base, but never friendly to the region. There are many issues to analyze. I think it is better to elaborate on a range of options that would be more relaxing for the parties. Let's see what proposal Kuper will bring. One thing is known, Serbia agrees to find a solution of Kosovo's representation in regional intergovernmental relations as soon as possible, so it is expected to find an agreement between footnotes, Resolution 1244 and ICJ.If there is no middle model, then this topic may also be called a failed one. Cooper has the situation in hand to propose a "medium" solution in order to avoid the ambiguity and incompatibility of the parties. Kosovo in no way accepts representation under 1244, and Serbia with the signature-Republic.

So there is not much left to hope that there is a solution to this topic. Let's see what the proposal will be, even though the international community has a label that it thinks may be acceptable, the term 'Kosovo'. But Serbian reactions to this topic are expected to be seen.

2.4. "Kosovo in the footnote"

Likely, but there are such ideas maybe interesting for experimentation but not real and actively segment of doing policy and made solution in international relation of states , just as important for practical solutions to problems between states it is not important to international policy of the state . It is very interesting that Kosovo in different relations in the region and beyond is represented in variants, perhaps strangely that there were international practices, or rather, the experience of solving problems among states. Such a proposal is quite "slim" as a proposal and perhaps loses functional logic in international reports. With such proposals because of a state, Serbia, to be played with some unconventional synonyms with the entire international community, and the latter through Cooper brokers to propose something like this, it is a daunting legal and international logic. There could be other functional logic without using the logic of footnotes because this "brings Kosovo to the seminar and scientific works". This is a short cut. But really no one has expected to have our state's participation in "scientific footnotes". Perhaps this interesting situation has other options for solution, but this proposed variant can hardly be found, or at all, in international reports. One is clear that Cooper has a good and noble purpose and according to him, maybe it does not matter whether Kosovo is in the footnote or other variants ..., it is important for Kosovo to participate in international developments without any difficulties brings Serbia. But even one issue is interesting, Serbia has the power to play this game in extreme variants, while the international community proposes various variants that will please Serbia. This also loses the logic and the correct understanding of international developments in the face of considerable recognitions of the state of Kosovo by many states.Another curiosity is that the political parties, the Kosovo Parliament did not once think "that this is a good act", to accept that our state is placed on the footnote? The invention and the development of the presentational state logic in this domain is a special curiosity, and we can say that there is no other creature in the international relations that can be treated so and so interesting. Or, maybe Kosovo is a unique "species", or a unique creature, and how it is dealt with in some international models or legal versions. Respect for Cooper's commitment to this "Balkan mess," but the suggestion would be; other proposals in this international relationship of the state of Kosovo through possible symbols such as: R. Kosovo, but without a footnote, only when Serbia or some countries that have not yet recognized Kosovo make problems, but not always, because this for us it is unacceptable to remain in this weird naming variant. Or how to say different treatment in a "single cage".It is of utmost importance that Kosovo be an integral part of all international forums, but should preserve the values and dignified treatment of our state, with local and international sacrifice and power, has been created. There are many things that can be said on this topic ... to hope to preserve the value and dignity of our state and the dignity of citizens, and to find an acceptable solution for our country.

2.4."Footnote" should be timely move in mean time only selective

The situation about representation in Kosovo's regional conferences since the government said "yes" strange formulas and reactions of the opposition parties and civil society with clarifying efforts to our friends not all agree on this representation of Kosovo through this model cause confusion to public opinion. For this reason, the representatives of the people - the Assembly of Kosovo are not asked at this time - they are not even at the event and play the role of citizens who voted for them - and they are not asked at all, but we have no reaction from Kosovo Assembly on this topic. While public opinion or citizens do not understand at all the meaning of this "footnote" that will be used "in place" and "improper" in written regional documents. The "flipchart" pattern, which has been neglected and unexplained sometimes in similarly similar situations, has created a state of confusion among citizens, while political parties are more informed, there is still confusion, why, what this means now? Finally, the diplomat Rohan said his op the remark in another dimension I emphasize that in the footnote to be written: not recognized by Serbia ". Rohan in this model as it is presented looks much more realistic and effective so as not to become any other state dam in Kosovo in wider representation.

2.5. Below I will mention some important segments of using the "footnote" 1. However, this is an unfavorable state of affairs in this model for our country, but the consequences should be minimized in size and instrument of action to be defined for a period of one year waiting for other developments that Serbia recognizes Kosovo.

2. Footnote and 1244 cannot be used at levels and representations other meetings in regional or international or only should be use where Serbia is participates on this conference, although Kosovo citizens is against any

mention of this resolution even because in Kosovo is impression that it is note more valid and important for Kosovo people .

3. Guarantees that the footnote will contain the declaration of independence and international recognitions that may be the number defined in the footnotes, depending on the number of states that may be added that recognition of the state of Kosovo is in continuity as well as the number of international financial organizations have recognized the state of Kosovo;

4. The mediator and the states of the quintile must ensure that this formula of representation is without any other legal and short-term consequences.

5. The EU should consistently support the integration of Kosovo into the EU and in this way the visa liberalization.However, there are many comments and even fierce discussions on this formula adopted by the Government, discussions are generating numerous comments and analysis as far as they are, the effect of the verb on citizens is growing not only with the parties and civil society. We all want to represent our state at any regional meeting but of course to the extent that it implies the state's dignity of Kosovo and its citizens. Institutional and operational maturity is at the level of the political parameters of unity, it is not the position of the party but in the future nor the other parties to deal with the national interest "only" that they are in power because the national interests exceed the narrow political parameters parties and that in each variant the dominance of the state of Kosovo should be dominated. There is no need for anyone to be protected or sheltered in "other chests" in such circumstances. It is necessary to preserve the level of responsibility and seriousness in these situations and to preserve the level and public opinion supporting the state lines and the national interest it has Kosovo to negotiate. Normal is not the idea of halting the dialogue but of the idea of EU political and integrative sincerity that conditions and circumstances should be the same for all countries aspiring to be part of the EU.

2.6. What does it mean for the state of Kosovo

This means continuing dilemmas in relations with Serbia and without normalizing the state of affairs between states, but only with attempts to find ways of fraud from Serbia or to investigate other political problems to prevent and blackmail and threaten Kosovo, or to lean in the same trend of development. The international community is currently losing its efforts and investments with Serbia to persuade him to do this or that? The Serbian positions are likely to remain unchanged and the only way for the international community to take other measures and pressures or, eventually, sanctions against Serbia, which at the moment has no discussion at all in the international community. This is why Serbia continues to behave the same and ever laugh at the international community with "soft but effective" tones in politics. Otherwise this policy is not distinct from Milosevic, but it only takes time, and if it continues, the international community will deal with Serbia for 20 years without any results on Kosovo. But if Serbia is well analyzed, there is not much pressure seriously from the international community to normalize relations with Kosovo, here is the Serbian game with barricades and other issues that have now completely lost the seriousness of the issue.

2.7. EU and promises behind footnote...

While the Serbian state is enjoying the recent agreement, the reason for why the state of Kosovo is awaiting the fulfillment of the promises made by the EU is well known. And if we analyze the current circumstances that have been created in the EU, when now the EU mentions and congratulates Kosovo and Serbia equally as never before in reaching strange agreements that have nothing to do with the practices so far recognized and appreciated as a political agreement but not interstate agreements that are of a type of respect for international law. The EU's policy and interests to Serbia, at any rate, give candidate status is also the key to pressure on Kosovo. But if we analyze further, the EU has promised, and these emerge as unsafe in the context of the rewards that Kosovo should have done for its foreign policy. The feasibility study says it can not yet begin, but it also says there is still no consensus on the subject in the EU. But even if this is still achieved we are far from European integration. With a negotiating team emerging from technical talks in totally unprepared political talks it can be said that this is a team that is really not capable and needs to be reconstructed altogether. At all analytical views that can be made of this, but this is still convenient because it is passive because it has no ideas and versions or models of solutions but relies on the EU's will and walking in the extreme ways between national interests and those regional and European level. Representation of Kosovo in these talks on the normalization of relations between Kosovo and Serbia is the lowest possible professional level, Edita with several assistants develops dialogue on very serious issues and unimportant, extremely important and political issues such as was the case of the footnote. So this is about to come true. Rather than seeing a range of proposals made by this team speaking on behalf of Kosovo, no models have ever been presented to the Government or institutions of Kosovo or even the Cooper, who have had to submit a range of options, then for what he talked to me, and there is not even a chartmap of guiding models for talks, considering the variants that represent the interests of the country, but this has done the mediator I said in one case the models are poor presented to parties that are between the line of failure and the success limit. Kosovo remains without the foreign policy itself fragmentation of this political one, it is strange that the Minister of the Ministry of Foreign Affairs is not part of this delegation, but in reality he mostly walks in a positive sense to find good ways to integrate Kosovo into EU or take another pearl of AKR President B.Pacolli who is lobbying and working for the recognition of Kosovo that has probably had little success, instead of being people in the talks there is someone else with assistants to negotiate. I cannot understand this by saying that there was no will for opposition people to be part of eventual teams called in these cases "unity", which has brought a series of problems and, in the end, problems of representation of regionally for a while with a footnote (footnote). This negotiating team has not done its job, unfortunately we have waited since this team "has it been" in the composition to present at least ten versions or models how Kosovo is presented at the regional conferences that was the most important issue since when these talks started in reality there was no opinion or opinion was presented to the local opinion. One issue, at the moment, without the content of the agreement, people of politics jump to generalize the representative formula of Kosovo , speak for both regional and general representation in the EU. While the EU is very cautious in topics such as representation in eventual EU conferences with this footnote or entry into other EU integration processes, and there is no single official position on this topic. Currently not even discussed this topic in the EU, we are now running the Minister of Foreign Affairs and the Minister for Integration .., to get the last minute reminded the Europeans that we have contributed to the agreement and remain loyal to European politics we ask for talks to be opened, feasibility study and the issue of visa liberalization begin. So far, we have not yet won anything from the compromise policy, perhaps in the coming days I will change European policy, at least all of those promises will be met by at least half. We remain to ask our friends US, UK, Germany France and many other friends make us out of a state of affairs, to make us possible integration and to find a dignified shelter in the European family. Will not be step away to discuss for that they say fo painful solution for our country. It is as it is, Serbia is likely to win EU candidate status and discontinue these talks that have become normal for the moment for Serbia's interest ahead of the elections there that were expected to be held . What's next ... is not known only there is a well-known issue to make the list of organizations that should join Kosovo, in that list there are also no organizations at all and convincing the public that the job is good. Should cooper stand out with a clear attitude about the last deal to show how? How? Where? How will Kosovo be represented only in regional conferences or in the EU integration process, is it a temporary interim formula. We strongly believe in the Western way of life and Euro-Atlantic development and integration in hopes of making positive changes in access to Kosovo's national and state interests in relation to Serbia and the countries that have not yet recognized us in negotiating teams , there is not much politics that there are many things that should only be guided by expert teams at relevant levels of talks to find the best ways to protect the interests of our state.

CHAPTER TWO

1.Agreements are a piece of paper

Recently, always in the prime minister's vocabulary - but also in the media - the term "agreement" is mentioned without specifying the type of "agreement". Some mention the word "treaty", and in reality they do not even know whether they deliberately say so or what they will say with this label! A part of them think that Serbia has already made steps to recognize Kosovo, while Serbia continually refuses this and does not mention such "agreement" names. They all speak of a kind of potential document that has nothing to do with international agreements or treaty types, which automatically came to recognize Kosovo. This seems to be a bit difficult to happen in Serbian nationalist politics when they are attempting to open a door to Kosovo's canton or other legal identity forms, or to leave the door open to any ethnic Serb political organization within the state of Kosovo. Many use terms that are related to the type of international agreements, but not so convincingly to our opinion, because things really are quite different: Serbia tends to have a worthless letter signed with Kosovo that does not show either form or international legal content, while for this or some kind of international agreement does not claim to be signed by the EU and US between the two states. This is more about formal acts built with a political language, demanding at any rate normalizing relations between Kosovo and Serbia, without prejudice to the type of potential document to be signed. There is no adequate legal-international terminology that could be mentioned directly. Thus, this position of the EU and the US stands for: the document may be formulated with requirements and conclusions that lead to solutions, but not by specifying the name and address of the document type that would otherwise prejudge a variant of recognition of Kosovo.A document in the form of conclusions is expected to be signed. In addition, the Belgrade side makes an effort to declaratively agree with the conclusions, without giving any strong guaranty that will be respected by northern Serbs. Meanwhile, neither the international statements are so decisive that Serbia has to sign something. This is attempted to be minimized. It is important to achieve the goal, so that the states normalize the reports: neither more nor less. This game is being played for a long time and the effect is most important. This is what the EU wants. Our side looks valiant and this is good for us in the face of pressures. The EU sometimes gives impressive statements to Serbia, that they have made progress on reforms in Serbia, but often praising Serbian leaders for compromise. On the other hand, senior Serbian officials play great words, supposedly they know a lot, that they are clear that Kosovo is different now and so on. Few to believe in this wordplay. Nothing more. Kosovo will remain for a long time in "frozen conflict" as a result of Serbian unwillingness to recognize Kosovo as a state. We all know that some sort of paper is expected to be signed, but we do not have to say that this is an agreement because it would not correspond to reality. Therefore, a confirmation letter is expected that the parties accept the conditions for normalization, without the name and address of any international document.This letter of confirmation means the opening of Serbia's door to the EU. Serbia should thank Kosovo, her neighbor, for a good job and good game, while Kosovo is not known what she wins. But it can be said that Kosovo is increasingly resembling a state of peace and regional prosperity! Now, Serbia will continue its game with Kosovo and other northern Serbs in other modalities. Whereas, Kosovo should continue to work to preserve territorial integrity.

1.1. A Agreement or any other document unidentified internationally, or only letter of confirmation between the parties

The term "agreement" is always mentioned in the prime minister's and medial dictionary, without specifying the type of "deal". Some mention the word "treaty" in reality, either they do not know or deliberately say so, do you know what they mean by this name? A part of them think that Serbia has already made steps to recognize Kosovo, while Serbia constantly refuses but does not mention such "agreements", they all talk about a kind of potential document that has nothing to do international agreements or treaty types, which automatically led to the recognition of Kosovo. This seems a little bit as difficult to happen in Serbian nationalist politics, where they seem to be making more efforts to put a door to Kosovo's cantons or other forms, or to leave the door or gate ready for any ethnic Serb within the state of Kosovo . Many used terms that are related to the type of international relations but not so convincing about our opinion, because things are really different, Serbia tries to have a worthless letter signed with Kosovo that does not show either form or international legal content, while for this or some kind of international agreement does not claim to be signed by the EU and US between the two states, this is more about formal acts constructed with a political language, seeking at all costs normalization of relations between Kosovo and Serbia without prejudice to the type of document possible signature, there is no adequate international legal terminology that could be mentioned directly, so this is EU and US position, the document may be type-formulated with demands and conclusions that lead to solutions, but not by name and address of the type of document, otherwise it would prejudice even a variant of Kosovo's recognition. A document in the form of conclusions is expected to be signed, in addition the Belgrade side is trying to declare only to agree with the conclusions but without giving any strong assurances that will be respected by northern Serbs, but international declarations are not so decisive that Serbia should sign something that is attempted to be minimized, it is important to achieve the goal, so that states normalize reports nothing more or more, this game is being overused for a long time and that the effect is most important this is required by the EU . Our side looks valiant and this is good for us in the face of pressures. Sometimes it gives even the impressive statement for Serbia that progress was made in reforms in Serbia, but it has often praised Serbian leaders that they are for compromise while senior Serbian officials play in big words, supposing they know much about it, it is clear that Kosovo has it is different, little to believe in this game of words, nothing more, Kosovo will remain for a long time in "frozen conflict" as a result of Serbian unwillingness to recognize Kosovo state. We all know one The paper is expected to be signed but we should not say that this is a deal because it would not corrode with the reality, so as I said a letter of confirmation is expected that the parties accept the conditions for normalization and without the name and address of any international document.

1.2. What brings the affirmation of the parties

This letter of confirmation means opening of Serbia's door to the EU, Serbia should thank Kosovo its neighbor for a good job and good game, while Kosovo is not known what it once wins, but it can be said that Kosovo is coming up more and more in a state of peace, regional prosperity. Serbia will continue its game further with Kosovo and with northern Serbs in other modalities. While Kosovo should continue to work to preserve its territorial integrity.

1.3.The document will be sent to Kosovo and Serbia with "take or leave"

The dialogue between Serbia and Kosovo in Brussels clearly indicates that there can be no dialogue on the territory and opening up opportunities to establish other autonomous units within the state of Kosovo, the Serbian side has once again demonstrated once again its real political face that it is interested for disintegration of Kosovo, but not for the normalization of relations between Kosovo and Serbia. It seems hopeless for the dialogue to produce a document of conclusions in the coming weeks.

1.4.The EU and the US will offer the parties "political ultimatum"

There seems to be no dialogue and formal meeting as Baroness Ashton said, there is only an ultimatum from the EU and the USA, the parties have at their disposal a time to eventually accept any agreement of conclusions, this should have been so, Ashton should to send to the parties a draft final conclusions on the "take or leave" position, this should be the epilogue, I consider that the last opportunity has been exhausted for the parties themselves to reach an agreement. Other routes no, everything is known, the Serbian nationalist side does not understand and will never understand the new reality in the region, it is still dealing with the nationalistic games of the past, if so, Serbia again finds itself before the capitulation, this time in the political aspect .Serbia wants disintegration of the state of Kosovo There are no other forms to reconcile Serbia, they want to disintegrate the state of Kosovo and do not recognize it as a state creature, this is the problem, the EU must be clear, it is time to tell Serbia that Serbia accepts the normalization of relations with Kosovo or there will be no integration of Serbia into the EU.

1.5.Kosovo and Serbs minority

Serbia again closed the way for itself, missed the chance to offer solutions to Serbs in Kosovo, if so, the northern Serbs will have the fate of the Croat in Croatia, which will be Belgrade's own responsibility. No desirable was the dramatic scene in Brussels created by the Serbian delegation, this proves once again that there will be no agreement with this category of Serbian politicians who are not interested in waking up from centuries-old dreams, severe dreams and dreams eternal has overtaken Serbia, it makes them realize that it is in vain to pray Serbia to become aware, not interested in awareness, are interested in the myths and legends created by the Serbs themselves for Kosovo, these myths and legends they turned into everlasting political and strategic programs, it shows something completely real that they do not have a place in the EU and cannot have their own future, seem to have been determined for problems in this century as well.

1.6.Serbia seeks new date for dialogue, this is futile

Regardless that they, Serbia had sought another opportunity for dialogue, I think it is useless to give up other opportunities for dialogue, they will never say any document of conclusions because their game is clear "only all or nothing "is different from the Serbian mentality, so I consider that it is time to make it clear again to Serbia, this also brings other things in international politics to think about what to do with the parallel structures in the north of the state of Kosovo , now the international community itself has to take the role in this area to find a solution for the parallel structures in the north.

What next

Silence before the day comes to Kosovo

In Kosovo, there is a "peaceful political" atmosphere, the Kosovo Prime Minister has informed me now of the relevant party and institutions with political and constitutional responsibilities of the country, and our path in this respect is clear - the EU document is acceptable to Kosovo the document preserves the integrity of Kosovo and solves the problems in the north of our country, and that more or less Ashton's conclusions are close to the attitude of the Kosovo delegation presented in Brussels, so it is a conclusion about these concepts drawn by Ashton, that is clear for all of us, even though Kosovo politics does not want Serbia to fail so another conclusion can be drawn, because there are things that also connect to Kosovo's future in the future when it comes to Kosovo's EU integration, so the responsibility of the head of Kosovo the state of our country is very aware of this. The Kosovo delegation last time in Brussels had done what could be done. What was wise to do in my analysis was done in Brussels, there could not have been more, because there are red lines of conclusions for which Ashton could not give up, it has made possible compromises for the parties, but I will no longer think about the ultimatum it has made to the parties. Serbia had initially made concepts that have nothing to do with normalizing relations with the state of Kosovo, but had other goals that their mathematical calculus translated in political terms it is irrational and impossible. We do not seem to do everything according to our political will to solve the life problems of Serbian citizens in the north, what we care about is the blood remains an integral part of Kosovo and that suffice to remove from the agenda the problem of the north. The Kosovar politics is and remains quite generous to understand the citizens of but their diving - the Serbs in the scenario of their total loss and the equilibrium with the Krajina Serbs seem unavoidable, but of course this is the responsibility of the Serbian state politic that sends the "Kosovo Serbs" abyss.

1.7. Serbia is in trouble with its nationalist policy

Serbia is in a chaotic state, in a political panic and under pressure, the Serbian Prime Minister has held meetings and will hold talks with all actors of the Serbian political scene on Monday, he also consulted Serbs outside Serbia, as well as representatives of the Republic Serb leaders in Bosnia, the only head of the church is that the Ashton EU controversy to discuss all of them, in order to reach a full consensus on the conclusions paper, they will discuss this topic Monday in Parliament.

2. Conflicts and panic - Serbian politicians more trust SNS Vučićic than the current prime minister

There is a big mess and panic in Serbia as a result of the encouragement of many years nationalist politics. Such long-standing nationalist Serbian nationalism will cost it a lot of money, starting with the logic and the relativism of consensus - it is difficult for all to agree that they have no other way than accepting the document's conclusions so that trying to make the full potential of internal dialogue with all sides only to avoid political dissatisfaction in Serbia will result not so well, numerous options emerged during these meetings of the Serbian political leader for the so-called Serbian national interest. The Serbian goal and strategy of negotiating to deliver documents that would disintegrate the state of Kosovo fail entirely, it is interesting to mention the vocabulary used by the political leader Serbian: on the one hand that they expect evil if they do not accept the document and the isolation, the reduction of economic aid and foreign investment, and on the other hand, there were numerous ideas that were rounded off in the very earliest acceptance of Ashton's document, the dim political rhetoric and the disaster that he had brought to himself Serbia has lost all the parameters of a European or integrative policy of Serbia in international structures, why so?The Serbian political leader could say yes to some sub-chapters or that some of the concubines need to be worked out and clarified. -Serbia has no choice but to save it from capitulation.Never got back from politics - Serbia will try to find its way even on Monday, not to say it is not the ultimate document "take or permit," everlasting Serbian dreams, nor can all international diplomacy melt away last in Brussels, a document of conclusions should be accepted by Serbia, even though there are ideas and there are analyzes there to accept certain conditions by writing the answer yes, but with some other subpoints that would support the Serbs there and would not imply that all Serbian politics fail and capitulate. They are preparing a document of conclusions elaborated by those who, according to them, would walk "on the top of the grindstone" without being cut, this seems impossible but they have no alternative, they would have to to accept such an important document would be to say no to the EU, but the time is moving and the recent deadline is approaching. this or that, "this is and may be the end of Serbia or the new beginning on the European path.

Who is afraid of next year more?

The April-April dialogue between Kosovo and Serbia has begun to frighten Serbia for its European future, but also hurtful of internal unrest in Serbia, and possible moves in the Serbian government, and possibly even extraordinary elections that could to be held in Serbia by the end of this year, such comments in Serbia are not to be neglected in the Serbian circumstances there while in Kosovo the situation is more stable no one still expects any weakening of the trust in the Government except the VV which has purposes to known to this dialogue. As the situation looks more stable on such a level, there are some protests for KEK that often have tendencies from some circles that they present differently but also with "other wind breeze" for other changes in governance, but 'there is nothing in this subject, such forms can not bring about changes because these people are not on these topics and they have no power nothing to change anything in governance in Kosovo. The Kosovo government from the dialogue with Serbia has its legal goals, of course to win this process of visa liberalization, but perhaps the opening of the road to win the seat at the UN, these would be our benefits from this dialogue. In the end, Serbia has also admitted that there is nothing more to Kosovo than that, it remains the normalization of relations nothing else. In Kosovo, no eventual moves are to be expected except for the contested legitimacy of the President of Kosovo without a vote that has have hindered the democracy of Kosovo, these other things have remained in the same developments, there is still stagnation in electoral reform and the constitutional changes that must end within the year. There are also 2 and 3 months left and start the political party to think about the elections local.Some surveys .... Some polls about the popularity of parties in Kosovo do not seem to be real, not in those quotas or percentages in the order, may be somewhat accurate PDK, LDK, VV, but the percentages as well have been adjusted and adjusted, so there is little believe in these polls. I think that all parties have lost their electorates because they are rooted in the general developments in Kosovo and the dissatisfactions that are present to the citizens, enough to make a self-survey with the people you are escorting with and you will not no support whatsoever about whether the people are satisfied with these political parties? The answer is more than no, I have the impression that we will still have a drop in the electorate, which can be called democracies contested by the citizens who does not find themselves at all in these developments, but political parties and people of their families have found quite a lot of employment in the embassy where not so, so it is hardly any fun in Kosovo with these developments, but the message is that the citizen has no address nor who to trust me? This is even worse. Dissatisfaction is great with the citizens with these developments but there is no way to come up with perhaps the desired quality for the citizens tired of economic underdevelopment, corruption, familiar policy and problematic justice, all of which are severely affecting life of the citizen in the state of Kosovo.

2.2.Opposition divided in Kosovo

In Kosovo it is not possible to unify the opposition, so it seems that there is not enough will to make the opposition politics seem to know that the party knows only to be powerful when they are in power in the opposite opposition, and this is strange because it does not it is known that the party is a pro-citizen or just who is in power, so this is not happening in Kosovo, because there is no quality in government.

-Local elections this year

If this continues, neither the local elections in Kosovo can bring any other quality to the life of the citizen, so very soon they went four years and did not see much change in any economic or social development, so if this trend develops and does not there are changes in the life of the citizen, then nothing of these elections that should be kept more because the election law is foreseen but nothing new can be expected even in these elections, citizens' expectations are being the same, have more economic development, prosperity and equal lives, and where there is no dominance for employment and personal prosperity.

2.3. Start of Implementing of Document with conclusions

The Kosovo-Serbia agreement for the north, opens the way for two states to integrate into the EU, each party has now made its own interpretation and favors that come out according to them, it is important that that document and its contents can not be altered and modified. "Pleased and contented" have now become the same, and those who disagree with this agreement have no alternative. We do not forget that neither party agreed to all the proposals, but each side has made the best possible for political gains so they let the two prime ministers of two states and Mrs Ashton understand.Even a Kosovo victory, and also a failure of Serbia in international diplomacy Serbia at the last moment made a positive step, little was the belief that Serbia would accept any variant of this agreement, normally all the variants proposed by the EU did not benefit or favor Serbs and targets of Serbs that were territorial to Kosovo and disintegration of the state of Kosovo, this seems to be the end, there is no longer anymore in this regard, it is expected that the parties will deal with implementation plans. It is not yet known that northern Serbs will cooperate in enforceability? The dreams of northern Serbs are melting in institutions of the state of Kosovo. Apparently there is no talk about the mechanism that will force northern Serbs to participate in the implementation of this agreement, Ashton will probably have this in mind, otherwise the northern Serbs will continue to play. implementation is left to be written by Mrs Ashton this is reasonable with the market that behind it lies the EU. While the difficulties seem to be in the north, if they persist in the disobedience of Serbs there then the main detail is difficult. Let's hope that there is no political behind Serbia, which is known for such deformities, but what is said in Serbia, Dacic and the Serbian state leader are shown to be consistent with enforceability. Let's see how it will flow.

2.4. Prime Minister Thaçi leads the document implementation committee with the conclusions reached in Brussels

While on the other side of Kosovo it is now clear that implementation is expected to be Prime Minister Thaçi so it is also said in Brussels, that probably Prime Minister Thaçi will be the chair of the implementation committee together with KFOR, EULEX.

-The agreement is a rational necessity and product of current Kosovo-Serbia developments.The agreement as a whole is a consensual and acceptable document for the parties not the best possible, thus defining the flow of this document, but the agreement does not contain the mechanism of what if the northern Serbs do not accept the document-based transformations with conclusions. Will there be executive power KFOR and EULEX in this direction to promote the implementation of this act document. It is not known whether the northern Serbs will cooperate in implementing this plan, they have purposes that may hamper the implementation of the document because have pre-recorded everyday every day things, firing barricades and similar games, the streets now need to are released and start thinking about the institutionalization of the municipalities. Serbian nationalist politics should be replaced henceforth with Western integration policy and that the time of Serbia's withdrawal is probably starting, the EU and the US are happy that Serbia has accepted such a document, which in the first place paves the way for us the EU and the EU structural funds, the economic aid proclaimed for Serbia and other forms of support to Serbia. There is only one point to agree that sooner or later there will be no alternative to recognize the state of Kosovo in any way and model, the recognition of the existing borders will now be important, now the EU and the US over time to think about the recognition that the parties should make the current borders, perhaps without prejudice to the opposing positions of the parties on the status issue, otherwise Serbia will continue to "make one leg" politically with the Serbs. the state of Kosovo. The normal agreement could have been more clearly and legally legitimate, although some points can be commented and interpreted in different models, as mentioned in point 5, point 9 and point 14 of the agreement, Kosovo should think legally and in full compliance with acts such as the Constitution and its laws, such as the one for local self-government, the European Charter for Local Administration and the Plan of Ahtisaari, to make the implementation of these conclusions, another point 9 is perhaps a topic for consideration, but it should be the best logical and intransitive model of Kosovo to implement such a thing, point 14 is also a topic of Serbia's to respect Kosovo, to be part of the UN, it is said that the parties will not hinder each other. Another is the plan and the timeline of implementation that will be safely drawn by Mrs. Ashton's experts or her advisers, there are points that can be implemented in certain time and trouble, but there is a need for longer time to be implemented and in order for the EU and the US to be satisfied, there is now a document required by the parties in the wake of many separate documents or agreements that are expected to be implemented, or are underway for implementation. Do not forget that this is a more political document that does not need to comply with the will of the two parties in full, this agreement is required to be implemented according to the requirements and the points presented in the document. I believe that the administrative office in the north will help, which is expected to convey all the important issues that need to be undertaken in that part of the state of Kosovo.For Kosovo and Serbia open doors to the EU. The EU's goal was this, to accept the agreement and to get the doors of two in the European integration, now the EU must re-use the negotiation to recognize the reality and the borders of Kosovo in full membership of Serbia in the EU, otherwise the owl Serbs evolve in the old political style. And it is positive that Kosovo on MSA.

19 April, 2013 -Kosovo Agreement –Serbia

1. There will be an Association / Community of Serb-majority municipalities in Kosovo. Membership in it will be open to other municipalities mentioned in the agreement.

2. The Community / Association shall be established by statute. Its dissemination will only happen through a decision of the participating parties. Legal guarantees will be provided through the applicable law and constitutional law (including 2/3 of the majority of the decision-making

body).

3. The Association / Community structures will be established on the same basis as the existing statute of the Association of Kosovo Municipalities, such as the chairman, deputy chairman, the assembly, the council.

4. In accordance with the competencies given by the European Charter of Local Self-Government and Kosovo Law, participating municipalities shall have the right to cooperate in the exercise of their collective powers through the Community / Association. The Association / Community will have full access to the areas of economic development, education, health, urbanism and rural planning.

5. The Association / Community will exercise additional responsibilities, depending on how they are delegated by the central authorities.
6. The Community / Association will have a representative role in the central authorities and for this purpose there will be a seat in the community consultative council. Accordingly, a monitoring function is foreseen.
7. There will be a police force in Kosovo, called Kosovo Police. All the police in northern Kosovo will be integrated within the framework of the Kosovo Police. Salaries will be provided only by the Kosovo Police (KP).
8. Members of the Serbian security structures will be offered from one place to the equivalent Kosovo structures.

9. There will be a Regional Police Commander for the four Serb majority municipalities (northern Mitrovica, Zvecan, Zubin Potok and Leposavic). The commands of this region will be a Kosovo Serb, nominated by the Ministry of Interior, from a list to be provided by the four mayors on behalf of the Community / Association. The composition of the KP in the north will reflect the composition of the population of the four municipalities. (There will be another regional commander for the municipalities of Mitrovica, Skenderaj and Vushtrri). The regional commander of the four municipalities in the north will cooperate with other regional commanders.

10. Judicial authorities will be integrated and operate within the legal framework of Kosovo. The Pristina Court of Appeals will establish a panel of most of its judges who will be Kosovo Serbs to deal with all Serb-majority municipalities in Kosovo.

11. A section of this Court of Appeal, composed of administrative and judicial staff, will permanently stay in the north of Mitrovica (Mitrovica District Court). Most of each panel in the above sector will consist of Kosovo Serb judges. The location of the respective judges will depend on the nature of the cases in which they are involved.

12. Municipal elections in northern 13. Energy and Telecoms discussions will be intensified by both sides, and will end on June 15.

14. It is agreed that neither party will block or encourage others to block the progress of the other side on the road to the EU.

15. With the help of the EU, an Implementation Committee will be set up by both parties.

Three Serbian Strategies against State of Kosovo

1. Serbia has a certain strategy, I consider that Serbian politics is moving in ways that can be considered dangerous to the territorial integrity of the state of Kosovo, if we analyze well Serbia seems to have two strategies separated from one another , the first is that Serbia requires slow fragmentation of the territory of Kosovo or total disintegration - according to this strategy the Serbian interest is not expressed to the north of Kosovo but also to other parts of the Serb-populated municipalities, this logic is simple for them realizing that they do not recognize the state of Kosovo nor do they intend, but seek that through negotiations to break apart pieces of the territory of Kosovo.

2. Second Serbian Strategy

The second strategy is also the search for Serbian autonomy in Serb-populated areas in Kosovo , as well as access to Kosovo's economic wealth, for example, they claim that it is necessary to talk about property ecclesiastical property and the privatization issue they seek for privatization of enterprises in Kosovo don 2000-2018, intertwined with the interests of earlier times and the economy of the past, they claim to take their share of the privatization process and other natural resources, mines, public sector, where Serbia counts millions of Kosovo's state to catch or to still by doing a such a politics , which is the Serbian condition for recognition of Kosovo, these are two Serbian strategies that circulate and justify Serbian politics towards the state of Kosovo at present.Serbian intentions will never stop. It is not inconceivable that Serbia's resistance to implementing the current agreement, on the one hand, seeking the consent of the northern Serbs to the subject of the agreement on the other hand, twist and misinterpret its meaning, and want through the implementation ground to benefit other things. Northern Serbia they still have the intention of Vučićic and want to convince Vucic that Serbian politics will work towards their own interests and Serbian national interests.

Third Strategy of Serbia

Serbian President Vucic has repeatedly quoted a "Historical Agreement with the Kosovo Albanians". The Serbian demand in this country is not entirely clear, the first in Serbia has an extreme political nationalism that Kosovo fully deserves its undisputed sovereignty or Serbian illusion, the second option for strengthening executive powers of the Association of Serbian Municipalities in Kosovo, the third agreement on the division of Kosovo territory on an ethnic basis. This option has now been proposed as a correction of the Kosovo-Serbia borders since 1974 which no one in Kosovo discusses with Kosovar Kosovo President Hashim Thaci continues to mention the correction of the borders, it seems that Thaci is playing a political game with political opinion in Kosovo. Anybody in Kosovo does not want to exchange territories with Serbia. No one in the EU wants the correction of the Kosovo borders - the Serbs - it is considered dangerous as well in Kosovo - has an assessment similar to the German Chancellor Merkel. There is no division or exchange of territories. There is an opinion that in such a dialogue never after the transparency of the two Albanian peoples - Kosovo and Serbian, so there are behind-the-scenes political backgrounds unknown to the Kosovar and Serbian public. Kosovo does not accept any option dividing its territory, is unacceptable and risky for the state of Kosovo and for the reign. The only solution remains the agreement for respecting the 1974 border of Kosovo -Serbia. This is a closed subject, as far as the Serb minority in Kosovo is concerned, this minority enjoys territorial and territorial rights. Ethnic and political, so there are additional mechanisms that can guarantee the Serbian minority that no one should take their rights   political and ethnic guaranteed by the Kosovo Constitution. The Kosovo Agreement - The final Serbia will consist of three first segments, the agreement should guarantee the borders of both states, and secondly, it must guarantee that Serbia does not prevent Kosovo from joining the UN and other international organizations, the guarantee that Kosovo Serbs will enjoy their rights and full freedom guaranteed by the Constitution of Kosovo is a third segment of agreements Kosovo-Serbia.

5. Kosovo strategy and options

Option one: Kosovo will not be separated, no exchange territories with Serbia.

The second option is the Association of Serbian Municipalities to be only a non-mandatory mechanism for municipalities with ethnic Serbs, is a voluntary mechanism of Serb municipalities without pressure to join this community.

Third option : Association of Serb Municipalities will have the right to guaranteed by the Ahtisaari Plan and the European Charter for Local Self-Government.

Fourth option: Kosovo should include in the final agreement guaranteeing the rights of Albanians of the Preshevo Valley with the maximum political, ethnic and territorial standards.

5.1.Politics of the state of Kosovo

While Kosovo's policy is clear, it wants to solve the problem of the north, but does not want to deal with Serbian dreams and illusions and frauds that Serbian politicians pursue. The international community should be energetic in resolving the problems in the north to stop Serbian abstractionist politics and should quench the dreams of northern Serbs that they have Serbian delays over the process of implementing the agreement Serbian efforts are such, there is no stalemate, but there are delays and time is on their side because they are in a diplomatic offensive towards Kosovo and for the moment it is accepted by some international circles this Serbian game, political advantages make use of walking always a step forward to convince the international factor that reality in Kosovo is not what they see, this is the game that Serbia plays. It seems that it is necessary or should be changed in the strategy, not so much, but in terms of setting the negotiating boundary, these negotiations Serbia wants to keep it alive forever until it realizes its national interest, this continues so because it is noticed from the interest shown that step by step do things to the devaluation of the state of Kosovo.

The time is for the north to stop such things because they even after their plan for the security of Serbs there in the north, the idea is to continue the same with the politics of degradation towards Kosovo and in calling for them to have internal problems in Serbia with its citizens because of Serbian dreams for Kosovo, these are issues that they want to reflect in front of the international community that they are having internal troubles. So is the situation, I consider that this agreement should be implemented as soon as possible and of course the border points for which Serbia will be discussed on other technical issues.The constitution may change after the Kosovo-Serbia agreement.Kosovo's Constitution will most likely be subject to change, not because it is such a requirement that there are many ambiguities, which in essence have, and as such there have been problems and could not be practically practiced, but also the legislation drawn up now the Kosovo Parliament was a part of problems and difficulties of implementation.When talking about the current constitution, there seems to have been a preparation to start the process of changing it. There are many reasons to approve the changes proposed by the working group but it seems that the stagnation is a result of the political nature not only domestic but also international. We all know or at least ours we know how the constitutional development of Kosovo has evolved since 2001 until the Constitution approved by the Assembly of Kosovo.The constitutional development of Kosovo was and remains very painful, what seems to be worrying is that there are individuals who say it is its drafters, considering that they are only persons who are consulted for making changes, mainly this game of constitutional development of Kosovo was guided by the international community which also consulted with the party of Kosovo, but also consulted with the circles of Serbia to draft a constitution that also reflects on the care of Kosovo Serbs. Serbia is even earlier and is now interested in dealing with Serbs in two segments, namely the constitutional rights of Kosovo Serbs and their security.Nearly the Serbian plan or Serbian strategy has had support from all international institutions or there has been some understanding in international circles. The international community has achieved its objectives by offering Kosovo independence while the Serbian minority rights and security. It is no coincidence that as well such themes The Constitution and the laws will change, nor is it strange in the first place, first of all the locals are interested to change or are urged to start changing the current Constitution not to enter into force but why not in the queue first to see the international community look at the interest of Kosovo's state institutions to offer change.The test is done now can be expected or eventually expected to be gathered comments from the Kosovo-Serbia agreement to approximate the positions and once all has been done then to begin building a new Kosovo constitution so far it was a transitional constitution so now it has to to be a new, more stable and timely constitution for the citizens. It was interesting and it sounded frivolous a meeting organized by Friedrich Erbert Stiftung and ISK when some people talked about each one and among themselves about the personal merit of drafting Kosovo constitutions historically while the rest provided information and nothing else, the truth is the other, the framework constitutionalism was drafted by Dutch expert Lemon and his team, while other local people received in conspiracy qualities had made comments and remarks that were never part of the then constitutional framework or just some of them being part of that framework, such as the result was resigned by two local consultants at that time, while the international community negotiated through diplomatic circles even with Serbian authorities not to forget the interest of Kosovo Serbs. This was the truth and the misfortune that neither then nor even now can we avoid. It is interesting to mention other facts or plans, since the current Constitution does not need to be changed because if the Kosovo Parliament approves the conclusions - the agreement with Serbia, it is automatically enforceable because the current Constitution clearly defines the priority of international agreements on domestic laws although legally this agreement with Serbia is not an international agreement but only a conclusion between the two states.

5.2. The international community measured against Serbia and the issue of the recognition of the state of Kosovo

The international community was cautious, a typical slow European but significant diplomatic diplomacy that is quite relevant and controversial on the ground issues are coming to being resolved. I unconditionally negotiated with Serbia, Serbia had very substantial and substantive conditions in the face of the Kosovo crisis facing the international community. Serbia was clear, she did not want to be conditioned by the international community but seeks the maximum for the remaining Serbs in Kosovo, Kosovo did not have the courage to mention and conditional Serbia with the Albanian lands in Serbia. There the OSCE had assisted the Albanians of the Valley to speak with Serbia, for no single result. The situation was suppressed between the two states without resolving the mutual problems. Serbia's goal has so far been to regulate a large part of the problems by securing the Serb minority in Kosovo with all the political and territorial rights. Serbs and their squads in Kosovo have an independent life inside Kosovo. The implementation of the Serbian association within Kosovo has thus achieved the goal of Serbian resistance in the state of Kosovo. This means that we are a people of peace even when it is in opposition to the state interest of the state, but Serbia does not seem democratic anymore or does not deal with human-civil-political issues. Serbia extinguishes its parallel structures and makes decisions about "its legal structure in Kosovo"

5.3. Rejection of illegal structures by the international community Serbia claims to "build institutions and bodies acceptable"

Serbia does not give up "Kosovo", despite the acceptance of the agreement, the old Serbia with the symbols of the semi-feudal state continues its game, leaving not comfortable Kosovo. "Without logical and meaningless" this is not done, but with certain purposes she is making "strange" decisions such as the decision to establish temporary bodies in the territory of Kosovo, without giving up at all from the feudal nationalist hegemony on her alleged rights. Serbia's two-way policy is its strategy from the beginning to accepting these talks, nor does Dacic's request to participate in the Serb elections in the north, because now Serbia is expected to have another advanced approach to sophisticated to Kosovo, the approach is known to the disintegration and devaluation of the state of Kosovo, while the static policy of Kosovo in its direction is to protect its independence to Serbia at all costs. Even though the international community does not impress this job at this stage does not mean that it will never impress, as with the barricades in the north, it is happening that the Serbian strategy is offensive to Kosovo. But at the same time one of the four deputy prime ministers of Kosovo declared that the parallel structures will be extinguished, we can agree with this, but Serbia wants "the legal structure built in Kosovo, slowly and safely, as far as it cannot be known.The international community if it wants to stop the trend of influence in Kosovo should definitely ask Serbia to establish an independent Kosovo in the existing borders, otherwise after the elections in the north is expected another dialogue to happen, there is a trend of developments, this seems "no way exit ". This offensive of Serbian feudal politics continues and will continue, that Serbs and their politics do not know anything more, that is known. They have never learned the job to stop, the port continues by testing variants on variants to find ways to influence Kosovo and its troll. It seems that Serbia has entered a long-term game that is seen with artistic and deceitful nationalist politicians in the West, supposing that they have lost Kosovo for the time being, this seems dangerous for the peace and stability of the region. It is not the order to find ways to normalized relations with Serbia because they are never interested in this work, normalization they see for their benefit will now cure, on the contrary they as politics are not so naive with the request that Serbs go to the elections in the north and accept the loss of Kosovo. Never once has Serbian politics so far accepted, nor is it expected when considering that Serbian dream dreams and permanent dreams and hypnosis is working for Serbs who have gripped this people is not easy to give up dreams mystical and century-old ghosts. But most importantly, the international community is to ask for any condition for Serbia to recognize the state of Kosovo very quickly. If recognitions happen, then these reports normalize as normalized with Croatia in the case of Kraina

6. Constitutional changes at the doorstep

It is finally expected to change Kosovo's transitional constitution, all the signals are, the changes made earlier are a good basis, I long before, especially when the working group on constitutional changes has finished, I have said these changes are not expected are done without agreement with Brussels and Belgrade, so it was reconstructed slowly, the international community had made such a scenario very early. It was not a coincidence why it was expected to decide what the locals are interested in changed the constitution? Now they know it, it is difficult to stop them because these things are all international investments, they are soon expected to invite these other politicians who resist shortly to say a few things why the constitutional changes must take place. And then these politicians who are most abundant in Kosovo will say good is, there needs to be changes that internationals are asking for, you know the condition is constitutional and electoral reform for integration developments. It is a surprise that in some media and in some TV people will come up with economics and election times and constitutional times, then people who are not aware of constitutional changes talk about it on TV has fallen to hear such people Commenting on the "little drive" style, is in crisis with days of what is happening or should I feel? Well the final is expected, there are two things to happen to Serbia to take a step to approximate the recognition of Kosovo in one variant soft and transitional, this is now being prepared, the scenario is not one-sided, in this regard but it involves both sides, must move forward with any result, I consider that this is positive. Even Kosovo will lose something Serbia so has been cooked the scenario, now someone likes this to someone not? Naturally that it touches us that is talking about our territory and for the territory of Serbia no. Serbia also has debts to Albanian parts in its territory. Kosovo needs a constitution that strengthens the state of Kosovo. Constitutional changes are expected to take place, Kosovo must have a constitution that defines state relations and meets the needs for a state constitution, but it is understood in benefits of strengthening the state, state integrity. Until now, the Kosovar side has changed the constitution, others have done so, foreign experts with their work, but I remember that there are people in ours who say we have made this constitution? And they were only consulted, and nothing more, but we were tired to show that they did work on it, but the truth was quite different, I once remembered in the constitutional framework two local consultants resigned when they realized that they they are not asked about that job, this has continued today so, at a different pace, but neither the electoral reform will be done according to local needs not only what the political parties say to us, their representatives do not know what they say they are already taught with many areas or with an electoral zone, all the work according to them is, this in reality is different and much more substantial than what one hears from them. Electoral reform with an electoral zone - it is simply so far so far it was an area, while the election law has many problems within its own, it can be interpreted in different variants and leaves behind the dilemma, but when it is not seen nor serious work in dealing with this law, it is a bad thing for us, we have been working on elections or we have been picking up for a long time with the choices we know very well but these out of the outside world who have been supposed to change of this law have left a wider dilemma, it is a surprise that everyone talks about this work, and never even in the CEC have any ...? But this is so in our country the weaker level and the poor quality of it professional and political thinking is bringing our society into big problems, many people who have not been able to find themselves in the party have been subjected to analysis and criticism, even to what they have They said they had established different economics and economists - with constitutional changes and policy development, that's right to express their opinions, but the problem is what are the legal studies and political sciences in this country ??? economists talk about constitutional changes, these things are studied by internationals know that there is no affirmative intellectual consciousness in our country but there are too much enthusiastic enthusiasts with big wishes, but right everyone has the right to express free thought but this is also affecting the awareness and public opinion that the citizen sees these people trying all the time to say something, reading literature about politics, democracy and the other. So much damage has been done to our country until now, there is no culture of genuine debate and professionalism but has "driven a little." Qualitative changes in the constitution are always needed, so the main fact is that this path of constitutional change is not today it is about two years ago, so things are coming now by classifying what should and what not to be changed in the constitution. Now, the constitutional text classifications have been made, the changes must start, and the conviction for change is easier than the political parties they have asked for this, now this is done .., no need to be surprised.

6.1. The EU calls for reforms to take place in Kosovo

Statements by senior EU officials that Kosovo should note significant progress is a specific segment as well as general. Some issues are clear on the need to record progress in public administration reform, stopping corruption, electoral reform, but there are still many other things that we need to do. Also, Kosovo is required to compile a comprehensive plan for the north. This inclusive plan must show readiness and determination to address the issue of the north. This inclusive plan is not finished as it seems and a draft or snippets of this draft are in the drawer of the Government but also the international community's consent is required. Completing the supervised independence of Kosovo is moreover a completion of monitoring the implementation of the Ahtisaari plan, because a flexible monitoring will actually work in the future as long as the state of Kosovo is not objectively strengthened and strengthened to protect its state sovereignty, which is currently KFOR. Prior to Kosovo there are a number of tasks to be undertaken to conclude that the international community issues a report showing progress. The EU praises the continuation of Kosovo-Serbia dialogue to continue and to issue new agreements that show interstate relations have improved significantly. Dialogue seems to go further and the EU and the US with this dialogue are looking to solve some details that are practical for consolidating relations between the two states. Compilation of a comprehensive plan will probably have the final but most important form very soon is to make it transparent to citizens, political parties and civil society. Actually, the contents of this document should be known. This document may contain: the north approach as an internal problem of Kosovo with its citizens because the EU and the US are interested in the solution within the legal system - Kosovo's constitution, even though the issue of the north in this variant without international support, no clear solution to the problems in the north can be achieved. This plan has the functioning of the rule of law and the socio-economic components and some other fragments or pieces that go towards the functioning of the state of Kosovo. One issue is that there should first be organized local elections by the state of Kosovo to see the functioning of the institutions of the Republic of Kosovo first. Within the scope of this international policy it can be noticed that there is an influence and a way of thinking of resolving the problems between Kosovo and Serbia. This approach has a breakthrough according to international officials whether it is fast or slow but needs to conclude with a conclusion that will consolidate the region. This path of the international community along the way requires Kosovo institutions to find models for progress in other sectorial areas in Kosovo. Kosovo's challenges are the progress of progress in stopping corruption. The state of Kosovo also faces other agendas to achieve more powerful progress in the country's economic development. Kosovo has stagnation of economic progress and this may represent the essential problem for the country. There is no economic reform or any document that could lead Kosovo towards the consolidation of economic development or to show hope to citizens that there will be social peace and prosperity in economic development. Reforming the country is a very wide-ranging problem, it is not simply too complicated and difficult, and there are many things that need to be urgently subject to reform. This reform can not be done quickly because the problems are more pronounced and have survived in the last few years and difficult to achieve progress in some sectors. The country's reform approach needs to be urgently added to the table to find ways to show that there is hope for the country to recover economically and that there will be no problems that are continuing and are not known last. However, much remains to be done in Kosovo. Kosovo's citizens want to see the country differently in development aspects and there are numerous dissatisfaction among them. Therefore, seriousness must prevail, and the will to find the best ways to consolidate the country. Citizens are not satisfied with the economic, social policies and generally the presented political quality and the extreme politicization of all areas of life. It is also urgently required a political reform of the parties that act in terms of providing a quality life for the citizens and the eyes this move should change the current approach to policy-making which turned into a bizarre "crafts" where everyone would like to deal with it because we see it profitable, regardless of professional skills or other inclinations. is to make it transparent to citizens, political parties and civil society. Actually, the contents of this document should be known. This document may contain: the north approach as an internal problem of Kosovo with its citizens because the EU and the US are interested in the solution within the legal system - Kosovo's constitution, even though the issue of the north in this variant without international support, no clear solution to the problems in the north can be achieved. This plan has the functioning of the rule of law and the socio-economic components and some other fragments or pieces that go towards the functioning of the state of Kosovo. One issue is that there should first be organized local elections by the state of Kosovo to see the functioning of the institutions of the Republic of Kosovo first. Within the scope of this international policy it can be noticed that there is an influence and a way of thinking of resolving the problems between Kosovo and Serbia. This approach has a breakthrough according to international officials whether it is fast or slow but needs to conclude with a conclusion that will consolidate the region. This path of the international community along the way requires Kosovo institutions to find models for progress in other sectorial areas in Kosovo. Kosovo's challenges are the progress of progress in stopping corruption. The state of Kosovo also faces other agendas to achieve more powerful progress in the country's economic development.

Kosovo has stagnation of economic progress and this may represent the essential problem for the country. There is no economic reform or any document that could lead Kosovo towards the consolidation of economic development or to show hope to citizens that there will be social peace and prosperity in economic development. Reforming the country is a very wide-ranging problem, it is not simply too complicated and difficult, and there are many things that need to be urgently subject to reform. This reform cannot be done quickly because the problems are more pronounced and have survived in the last few years and difficult to achieve progress in some sectors. The country's reform approach needs to be urgently added to the table to find ways to show that there is hope for the country to recover economically and that there will be no problems that are continuing and are not known last. However, much remains to be done in Kosovo. Kosovo's citizens want to see the country differently in development aspects and there are numerous dissatisfaction among them. Therefore, seriousness must prevail, and the will to find the best ways to consolidate the country. Citizens are not satisfied with the economic, social policies and generally the presented political quality and the extreme politicization of all areas of life. It is also urgently required a political reform of the parties that act in terms of providing a quality life for the citizens and the eyes this move should change the current approach to policy-making which turned into a bizarre "crafts" where everyone would like to deal with it because we see it profitable, regardless of professional skills or other inclinations.... economically tired and nationalistic surplus. Serbian politics should show greater commitment to international policy developments in order to maintain the balance of development. Part of the EU obviously means respect for the European state order, which is normal for Serbia to recognize that Kosovo is an independent state and that it should be normalized interstate relations to move to European integrations. Whether Serbia will revive and whether it will change in international politics is expected to be seen in this newly started.

The EU requires pragmatism for Balkan states for its integration processes It is now seen that there are many segments that relate to issues of EU candidate membership, to full EU membership, this is very clear for all aspiring or dreaming states in the EU. These dreams of the Balkans perennial can be met with certain and often rigorous conditions. This is not easy for all Balkan states that have many problems from different from the functioning of the law and the law, fighting criminality, corruption, and relations between neighbors someone less and some more trouble around the integration process but above all is lacking the added awareness of these states aspiring to this will. The conditions that the EU exacerbates greatly impede this. Creating the conditions and circumstances of a stability internal is difficult when considering the problems that are present in Balkan states Albania that has to meet 12 conditions, Kosovo that could set conditions for solving the problem of the north of the state, so Macedonia faces a series of issues that also link stability and order and law and ethnic issues, Macedonia is having problems that are the natural nature of the substance, of course the obstacles coming from Greece in the integration process are very dense and controversial for many segments. The demand for finding the right path and solving the problem with Greece is the main concern of Macedonia. Macedonia is not finding a language of reasonable communication with Greece so that its integration is a normal process, it is a kind of blockade for Macedonia's integration status or integration status until full membership in the EU. The European policy must be clearer in this direction and I found the pattern acceptable to overcome the current political problems with Greece for which state is considered to stop Macedonia. The EU has the good will of Macedonia's integration despite the unilateral Greek will that has reasons and motives of historical-political nature, in these circumstances create difficulties and no objective pragmatic communication willpower and language. It seems that the policy of the state of Macedonia led there in the joint governmental policy faces some serious inability to overcome the integration crisis. This situation can be described as an overthrow of the integration process. Macedonia is increasingly becoming in a good way in finding of the model that will not be hampered by Greece. It should name an emissary for finding the road to Macedonia's EU integration, and NATO which will accelerate the achievement of any compromise in its notion because it has begun to lose weight especially a part of the Macedonian politicians and the Macedonian party that the isolation is happening for other reasons. For that time, we have the increase of the Macedonian influence on the Albanians there, perhaps all the idea of Macedonian politics is sensitizing the situation there and the internationalization of Macedonia's problem found a way out by add international politics. So the issue of Macedonia's emerging solution should be oriented, where Greece would not interfere with the integration process. It is necessary to find a model to unlock the current situation there by finding a non-refractive variant by Greece at the same time to protect the EU principles. Possible models may vary the following:

-Executive EU solution, by assigning a special emissary that would result in a model;
-Model of name avoidance Macedonia with shortened denominations MKD only for the Greek contending country;

This debate and this topic seems to be very dangerous for the region, given that the Western Balkans is full of historical and ethnic problems, but also in Europe has covered such topics and interests but that the EU has not even accepted even debate of this level for some countries with ethnic problems. Kosovo as an international status quo seems to be the "Sui Generis" experiment and international politics on ethnic issues. The different regional autonomies in some European countries have not brought solutions, while the model of not mentioning the notions and legal denominations at this stage is the best variant to solve historical and ethnic problems, exchange themes and debate on territorial exchanges is one the absurd topic, so this seems to be a preparation for that historic agreement that Serbia cited with Kosovo. "border correction is a return to the old history of a state that no longer exists. "Actuality at this stage is the result of Thaçi's ongoing lack of transparency and ignorance of Kosovo's intelligence. "Its own has capped" in this dialogue and did not interest anyone what it says or what it thinks. This stage seems to appear to have been ineffective, even though the EU has not been involved in the debate, the parties have been able to choose and even solve problems in this dialogue. "Serbia is trying the absolute maximum victory." Realistically this is very dangerous as an idea, a bit scary for bargaining with the ethnic territories that can be said, Serbia tends to break through KSA, almost 30% of Kosovo's territorial diagonal territory where Serbs live while Thaci mentions Presevo. So do not believe this is a good idea because the exchange opens many dilemmas in the Western Balkans even in Europe. These debates endanger Kosovo's statehood, constitutional order and minority policy in southeastern Europe, as functional state sustainability is being questioned.And while the topic, the historic and ethnic debate with Serbia is opening for the final agreement that is more convenient in each variant of Serbia than the poor and economically undeveloped Kosovo and the anarchic rule that Kosovo faces in the face of the lack of functioning democracy. "his debate and this topic seems to be very dangerous for the region, given that the Western Balkans is full of historical and ethnic problems, but also in Europe has covered such topics and interests but that the EU has not even accepted even debate of this level for some countries with ethnic problems. Kosovo as an international status quo seems to be the "Sui Generis" experiment and international politics on ethnic issues. The different regional autonomies in some European countries have not brought solutions, while the model of not mentioning the notions and legal denominations at this stage is the best variant to solve historical and ethnic problems, exchange themes and debate on territorial exchanges is one the absurd topic, so this seems to be a preparation for that historic agreement that Serbia cited with Kosovo. border correction is a return to the old history of a state that no longer exists. "Actuality at this stage is the result of Thaçi's ongoing lack of transparency and ignorance of Kosovo's intelligence. "Its own has capped" in this dialogue and did not interest anyone what it says or what it thinks. This stage seems to appear to have been ineffective, even though the EU has not been involved in the debate, the parties have been able to choose and even solve problems in this dialogue. "Serbia is trying the absolute maximum victory." Realistically this is very dangerous as an idea, a bit scary for bargaining with the ethnic territories that can be said, Serbia tends to break through KSA, almost 30% of Kosovo's territorial diagonal territory where Serbs live while Thaci mentions Presevo.So do not believe this is a good idea because the exchange opens many dilemmas in the Western Balkans even in Europe.

These debates endanger Kosovo's statehood, constitutional order and minority policy in southeastern Europe, as functional state sustainability is being questioned. And while the topic, the historic and ethnic debate with Serbia is opening for the final agreement that is more convenient in each variant of Serbia than the poor and economically undeveloped Kosovo and the anarchic rule that Kosovo faces in the face of the lack of functioning democracy. Territorial exchanges are disadvantageous to Kosovo and dangerous for the Balkans and the EU. "Serbia is trying to get ten Kosovo municipalities, but now this logic seems dangerous and damaging to the state of Kosovo. Therefore, it is not worth the debate to be made on this topic as Serbia is not interested in the exchange of three municipalities between the states but the 10 Serbian municipalities in Kosovo, proportion 10 to 3 in Serbia's favor, is not worth the least debate normal alternatives and Thaci scholars and his ignorance of the state or of the international legal order did not spur such endless topics and could cause dissatisfaction in Kosovo and other things that can hardly be managed by Kosovo citizens "These issues are occurring due to the lack of knowledge and the lack of creativity in resolving the rights of the Serbian minority, although this was actually solved earlier with the Ahtisaari plan. "Encouraging the problems of this extreme nature is the biggest mistake Thaci has made in political negotiations and has not respected the international agenda for technical issues approved by the UN. It should not be said about exchanges or breaking the state legal order of Kosovo, because it endangers the state and completely defunts Kosovo. Then Kosovo can be as independent and can join Albania but it does not have any international and regional weight for Western Balkan history.

7.Free interpretation for: "Agreement of the Association of Serbian Municipalities"
1. Summary of Facts:

Kosovo has a constitutional order based on the two currently-guided formulas:
a) sui generis formula

  b) Affirmative law for minorities

If we use the methods to establish the legality of the legal norm or the Latin "ratio of the leg" through the use of interpretations in this situation, we will take the truth of the norms of this agreement as follows: we should use linguistic interpretation in the original text in English, then it should be served with interpretations as follows: logical, evolutionary, purposeful and systematic. Based on the linguistic and logical interpretation of the constitution of the country the constitution - the part of the international conventions on human rights and the observance of these international conventions from Kosovo the assumption of obligations hence the embrace of the formula: affirmative European law and constitutional articles as follows: Chapter II Article 21, Article 22, Article 23, Article 24, 26, based on Article 124 of the Constitution, are also issued the following laws: Law on Local Self-Government, Law on Inter-Communal Cooperation, these laws derive from the European Charter for Local Self-Government accepting the affirmative formula for minorities and establishing a system of positive discrimination for minorities as an integral part of its constitution. The "agreement" for the "association" is built based on the 2013 agreement ratified in the Kosovo Assembly. Kosovo's constitution is transitory and in difficulty offers modern approaches to interpretation and quality standards that must have a modern and contemporary constitution. Kosovo has a sensitive or tangible constitution for respecting contemporary standards and has transitional norms. The association is an undefined body with defective definition based on logical interpretation and that intentional interpretation emerges as an uncompleted and non-finalized institution, its legal status should be defined to clarify its work and it is just an administrative body. The agreement is in accordance with Article 19.2 of the Constitution (citation ratified international agreements and legally binding norms of international law prevail over international laws (the Association Association Agreement is in line with the 19 April 2013 agreement ratified by the Assembly of Kosovo. Interpretation

Legal Act and Association:

"Association of Serbian Municipalities" (Use of the following interpretations: linguistic, evolutionary, intentional and systematic interpretation)

"Association of Serbian Municipalities" is a mechanism or administrative body with powers of oversight, coordination and development for the administrative fields mentioned in the following conclusions document: social issues, education, health, economic development, spatial planning, environment and environment and do not contradict Article 44.1 of the Constitution (freedom of association) and Article 124.4. Supervision implies the effective implementation of the objectives of the association, namely its statute act and decisions, common regulations. The issued acts are of a administrative nature. The Association also monitors the implementation of its objectives in the territory of municipalities that exercise some common competences. The Association may also exercise additional powers that may be delegated to it while maintaining the purpose of its establishment. The Association provides administrative services in the areas designated for the citizens of these municipalities in accordance with the laws of Kosovo (Law on Local Self-Government and the Law on Inter-Municipal Cooperation and other laws. The Association can enter into relations with associations of other local and international communes (Article 124, paragraph 4 of the constitution - cross-border and cross-border cooperation) as a "specific administrative body" (based on logical and intentional interpretation), can construct reports and other relationships from the areas that have or can be delegated by the central authority. To appreciate: to evaluate the quality services performed and to improve the quality of the services provided. The Association takes measures: in accordance with its activity it takes measures to improve the situation in the administrative areas.   Association of Serbian Municipalities structure (only a few important segments)."Association" has neither executive nor legislative competences (does not issue laws or executive body), does not contradict the constitution with article 4 and points 1-7 of this article. . Association of Serbian Municipalities issues applicable decisions to its members. The president of the association represents in the country and abroad for the mentioned common areas and competencies (logical interpretation). The establishment of "civil service" should be in accordance with the constitution with article 101 - replaced with the title "secretariat". Establishment of joint-venture companies: in accordance with the constitution and the law on inter-municipal cooperation. Relationships to ASK with central authorities KAS (item 11 of the agreement) may represent the interests of the municipality in the Constitutional Court in accordance with Article 112, point 4 of the Constitution (municipalities may challenge the constitutionality of laws or acts of the Government that violate the municipal's responsibilities or reduce municipal revenues in if the municipality is affected by that law or act.

Conclusion: The name "Association of Serb Municipalities" is not in accordance with Article 124 (Organization and Functioning of Local Self-Government) and is not in compliance with Article 16 (the supremacy of the Constitution, the name of the agreement contradict Article 81, point 1 , 2,3,4,5,, 6,7,8 (Legislation of vital interest), this designation does not comply with the standards of this Constitution. Kosovo Constitution based on Article 81 has defined the part of vital laws for which cannot be subject to a referendum. This implies, based on the logical, free and connected and evolutionary and systematic interpretation that: the name "Association of Serb Municipalities" is not in accordance with the constitution, municipalities based on Article 124 of the Constitution have no reference ethnic.Additional clarification: The Constitution under Article 124 abrogates the right of municipalities to formulate such designations for the implementation of the law on local self-government and the law on inter-municipal cooperation through such designation. Proposal: This association should be named: Agreement for Cooperation between Municipalities ...... based on Article 124.4 of the Constitution.

II.
The denomination in accordance with the constitution is suggested: "Inter-Municipal Cooperation". The following are the names of municipalities….The agreement is in accordance with Articles 58, 58 and 58.5 of the Constitution of Kosovo. Additional clarification: "Association Agreement" - does not conflict with the articles of the law on inter-communal cooperation, this law is in line with the Kosovo constitution and

allows for inter-municipal cooperation including the establishment of joint public enterprises (section 9.1.4), as well as the establishment of a joint administrative body Article 9.1.2). This agreement does not contradict Article 22, paragraph 1 to 8 of the Constitution, neither under Article 53 nor Article 59, paragraphs 1 to 14 of the Constitution.   The agreement is in line with Article 7 of the constitutional (democratic values).Based on Article 101, Paragraph 1 and 2, the Republic of Kosovo has a unique civil service and that only two levels of power have the right to recruit civil servants and fund this service.

7.1. Even Albania against the exchange of territories Kosovo-Serbia

The Albanian state policy does not support any kind of change of boundaries or delimitation of borders because of the possibility of a Balkan crises . Nobody has the courage in Albania to support Thaci's idea of border correction, very strange as a ideas and debates to develop in this period according to development . Who believes Thaci no one in Kosovo, Thaci and Haradinaj they are a same , they was divided because of personal interest , its better to have one political party.

7.2. Public opinion in Kosovo

Nobody in Kosovo thinks that it should swap territories with Serbia and make historical corrections of borders, it is true that once the Presevo Valley, Bujanovac and Medvexha were and are still ethnic Albanian territories, but in the former Yugoslavia, Kosovo's were three communes with the Serb population and three Albanian municipalities are given to Serbia, but now there is another reality, but no one yet backs Thaci into such ideas and adventures in Kosovo. Thaci remains a serious politician as Haradinaj both in the public the public have a definition that they are not for politics, but because of the recent war they have become politicians and they have not dreamed about getting such public positions before. They have not dreamed of taking such public positions. Kosovo has been demanding political changes in state government, a fast and strong alternative to join the EU and NATO, which are universal goals of Kosovo's citizens. n Kosovo there is a political turmoil and a great deal of how the state of Kosovo will be governed by both of these and the current parties. LDK, PDK, VV, NISMA, AAK are not politically alternatives for Kosovars, Kosovars are looking for something new generous generations to lead the state. There are many criticisms from new generations in Kosovo in that direction, they are demanding changes and alternatives where politicians will not benefit from the state but will work for the state, order and law, and to serve to citizens. The transformation of the government seems to be problematic because all the state sector's is control by people who are called untrustworthy and uneducated that the state should not be understood for personal interests but for the interests of all citizens. Thaci and Haradinaj are called in Kosovo as a uneducated, and this is growing and growing as a conviction in Kosovo. While the LDK is a party losing its impact on the populous due to its lack of readiness and political courage to make changes in the state and to make big decisions, LVV is a party without education and political opinions as well as with no ability to but it is hoped that this road will be located by its citizens, which is the engine of change in the state. The Kosovo people do not trust PDK, LDK and LVV and AAK and NISMA , these political parties have been shown to be problematic and they have done one thing against each other to take government in the country, so they have lost faith in Kosovo. The people do not think that these parties can hold a dialogue with Serbia in favor of Kosovo's interest, until these parties have been shown to be unable to make dialogue and to represent Kosovo's interests.

7.3. Failure to reach a political consensus in Kosovo

For the Kosovo-Serbia dialogue there is too much criticism for   political approach, the opposition in Kosovo does not agree with the leadership of the Thaci in the dialogue with Serbia, often there are many criticisms and they also demand Thaci's departure from the dialogue, which opposition parties in Kosovo has conclude a long time ago   as non-adequate person, and they request to establish team by Kosovo Assembly   . Kosovo's opposition parties requires a new elections an other hand has been said that by 2019 will be a final agreement Kosovo- Serbia at least international community have a such a expectations- to be reached final agreement..

-Serbia and medieval politics will not agree with Kosovo expecting other international developments

Serbia, according to the medieval political logic and based on nationalism and the conquest of the territories in the Balkans, will not easily be compared with the Serbian nationalist warrior for larger territories for Serbs, the Serbian war will not fail, and never ceased during the various Balkan developments, the biggest problem will be the final reconciliation. This dialogue, which started for 7 years, will not have a final solution, but a transitional solution and will continue the Serbian settlement in the Western Balkans.

7.4.European Union and opportunities for correction of Kosovo-Serbia borders

Until now, the European Union has not stated about Thaci's opinions on border management, the EU does not have any official position, except for Germany, which has stated that there is no exchange of territories between Kosovo and Serbia.So far the EU does not support Thaci's adventures, this would be damaging in both Kosovo and the EU. Kosovo is becoming non serious state in Thaci's proposals. In international law there are rules, Thaci seems to have only the himself rules This theme seems to be merely a topic for writing books, because the theory and reality are different, sometimes the new reality and circumstances may be not based always on international law or international legislation, resolutions and conventions. Thaci is known for adventure in the absence of proper political education, he usually opens up topics and and runs them two week a get close dependent to the local and international level, so it is known for opening the topics and get closed. Thaci's proposals such as the establishment of the Kosovo Army which took two week debate and get closed. Will idea of Thaci for correcting borders have the same fate as all the initiatives of this man during the last years which are so many we should have a passion to know ! The EU is very sensitive when it comes to borders matters , so this adventurer will not happen if should be asked German Chancellor Merkel. So far, there have been some international researches and civil society organizations that have been researching this topic and the possibilities for the happenings, but have remained only at the level of analysis or school research. France and other EU countries have no standing on this topic, so Europe will stop Hashim Thaci's dream of correcting borders in the Balkans, and this is also a problematic issue when we talk for the circumstances of how these states are function in Western Balkans. is of great importance for the coming period and the time that Kosovo-Serbia dialogue is to be concluded, which is proposed to close in 2019, possibly with the solution and normalization of relations between the two states. Ahtisaari plan made a Kosovo as a multiethnic state, although 90% of citizens are Albanians with small   other minorities, but this plan offers protected cultural and ethnic areas of Serbian minority , who were privileged beyond measure and need. Ahtisari plan made Kosovo- state, " but today" there remains a problem of functionality in municipalities where Serb minority lives in all over Kosovo. Ahtisaari's plan was generous plans so far proven but not even researched, Ahtisaari's plan was clear, Kosovo cannot be divided, cannot join anyone and there is no change of boundaries.

8. Who did not like Ahtisari's plan?

Serbs and Russians do not like these plans, and why Serbia wants a division of Kosovo, as long as it likes the continued political rivalry with the West. Serbia remains a major problem in the Balkans, which continues to support Russian politics ever openly against Kosovo and the EU and US states. Serbian nationalist politics has been directed against the Balkans that sometimes this regional state feels itself strong in the Balkans and within the developments within. The Russians want a troubled and unmanaged Balkans coming from Western states. Serb politics is clearly left against the state of Kosovo and against the US. Russians through Serbia want to keep the unsure and curious Balkans in Europe, Russian politics works more than a century in Balkan developments. Russia does not care about the normalization of relations between Kosovo and Serbia, but its interest in Balkans through Serbia, the political problems in the Balkans have not stopped, while Russia has so far not given any commissions for Kosovo partition or border correction in While Serbia's undisputed politics calls Kosovo and its institutions as temporary, Serbia is a nationalist state, a hegemons who has never experienced historical relics and lives with myths and fables, often the losses of the Serbian state. this state calls it as a winner, without logic and sense , but it is Serbia of the Middle Ages and of today as well, not changed at all in politics and international relation..

8.1.US opportunities for correction of Kosovo-Serbia borders

US for Kosovo-Serbia border corrections have stated that this is a matter of parties in the dialogue. Serbia and Serbia have enforced the borders of the former Yugoslavia since 1974, which at the time of the former Yugoslavia were called administrative boundaries. The US has not commented more nor with Thaci's declarations for border correction. The US statement is of special importance for finding a friendly political solution for a future of the two states, a viable solution must be found even though little is confident that there will be a lasting solution, a viable solution is possible while the final solution is difficult and unpredictable. The US has a major role in the Western Balkans and has an impact on Kosovo's foreign policy, so far the United States is the most important strategic partner of Kosovo, the US partnership - Kosovo is great in the Western Balkans.

CHAPTER THREE

BLERIM BURJANI – statements

(DOUCHE WELLE)

International obligations and support

Political analysts the messages of the vice president interpreted as messages that Kosovo should perform international obligations, whether they like it or not. "The demarcation with Montenegro should be implemented according to obligations assumed by Kosovo-Montenegro, signed in Vienna in 2015. The ratification of this agreement should be made through reaching a consensus but also with an emphasis on the opposition and Demarcation is an international condition set for Kosovo. It likes or dislikes someone, this demarcation has now gained international support, "DW told analyst Blerim Burjani.

How Compromise Is Possible?

But how far is it possible in these circumstances to compromise between Kosovo and Serbia, to reach a final settlement agreement? Blerim Burjani, political analyst told DW that the parties' intentions are already known, Kosovo aims at a UN position and finally recognition from Serbia, while the latter through the Serbian Association of Serb Municipalities seeks for partition within Kosovo's territory."Now the compromise is problematic for both sides. Kosovo cannot be fragmented and become a non-functional state, even though Serbia claims that the association is completely independent of Kosovo's institutions, "says Blerim Burjani. According to him, Serbia intends to partially fragment Kosovo through the Association, and this happens later if the Kosovo side accepts with these conditions "the historic agreement with Serbia." "Serbia wants a mild separation, as a variation, where Serbs will to have treatment as a separate legal entity, as defined by the working group for drafting the Statute of the Serb majority municipalities. In it, the Serbs themselves independently determine their free will of Pristina. On the other hand, Kosovo has requested that this statute be controlled and supervised by the Constitutional Court of Kosovo. So even Serbia has an advantage in this topic as a proposer, then it remains to Kosovo to declare for this and that Kosovo politicians leave this topic politically by sending it to the Constitutional Court to get rid of the debate about "betrayal" and other things. So compromise with Serbia in these circumstances seems impossible, "says Blerim Burjani.

Dialogue with Serbia

Another political connoisseur Blerim Burjani tells DW that Kosovo in the decade of independence is still on a path to consolidating state institutions. "The main challenges of Kosovo remain the strengthening of the rule of law, in particular the functioning of the justice system, the fight against corruption, nepotism, the spreading of full sovereignty in the north of the country, the establishment of the Armed Forces, the implementation of the Agreement on the Association of Serbian Municipalities , the ratification of the demarcation with Montenegro, visa liberalization, economic development and health and social protection and European integration, "says Blerim Burjani, adding that Kosovo needs a greater push from the EU in terms of giving the will to integration processes. "So the EU should more encourage and give willingness to Kosovo's institutions for integration processes. The EU should support more Kosovo citizens, they need greater EU support not to be isolated from Europe. Kosovo's citizens remain loyal friends of the EU and the US. Kosovo citizens strongly believe in the EU and its developments, because Kosovars are committed to the path towards European integration. The EU should offer more will to Kosovars, "says Blerim Burjani.

The new government after the elections

"These elections are unattractive, nonprecious for the citizens. Youth is conscious? When they can not find themselves in Kosovo, they are applying to leave the state. Numerous profiles have fled and are fleeing for a better life: professors, doctors, engineers, singers, artists and everything else. Kosovo is still the only country that is benefiting from politics, "says Blerim Burjani. He says the turnout of citizens will be the biggest challenge for Kosovo."How to vote to recycle corrupt and personal beneficiaries. How to vote for people who have raised pensions for MPs and have increased salaries and have passed laws that if they are no longer in politics, they can return to where they were, to work in the civil service of the state. But who would be involved in the Western world with this category of people. Kosovo citizens should be aware of who they are giving the vote, "says Blerim Burjani. According to him, the acceptance of results and the formation of the Government should be done through mutual consultations, dialogue and mutual understanding. The demarcation consensus is also a sign for other major decisions.

International obligations and support

Political analysts the messages of the vice president interpreted as messages that Kosovo should perform international obligations, whether they like it or not. "The demarcation with Montenegro should be implemented according to obligations assumed by Kosovo-Montenegro, signed in Vienna in 2015. The ratification of this agreement should be made through reaching a consensus but also with an emphasis on the opposition and Demarcation is an international condition set for Kosovo. It likes or dislikes someone, this demarcation has now gained international support, "DW told analyst Blerim Burjani.All these developments and messages do not convince the opposition to give up the controversy of the demarcation with Montenegro and force the Kosovo government led by the chairman of the Democratic League of Kosovo (LDK) Isa Mustafa to enter into a confidence motion in parliament. With a majority of votes, the government Mustafa lost confidence and Kosovo went to extraordinary elections in June 2017. After the elections, no political party took the necessary majority to make the government itself, but after joining a coalition of Ramush Haradinaj with the party (AAK), Kadri Veseli with his party (PDK), and Srpska list with official Belgrade support, Ramush Haradinaj, is elected prime minister of Kosovo.

Word Games that Lead to Cramp

The political analysts see these developments completely unnecessary, reflecting the stubbornness, the play of words and anger of political subjects. Blerim Burjani, a political analyst, says the constitution has made it clear who belongs to the chairman of the assembly, while for the government says he needs political agreement. "The Speaker should be elected as soon as possible, the opposition is not able to choose who will be the mayor, it is proposed by the PAN coalition, because it is the winner of the elections, and this is permitted by the constitution of the state, therefore there is no need to make opposition politics. Burjani points out that regarding the election of the prime minister, Kosovo needs a consensual prime minister, prime minister of political compromise, another prime minister (since Vetevendosje and LAA are against Haradinaj), even outside the position and opposition a credible person for several months so in order for the state to function normally until other elections, otherwise Kosovo is in deep political stalemate, "says Blerim Burjani.

The result of early June 11th general elections did not yield any winning political entity that could only elect the speaker of the assembly and create the government of Kosovo. The national presence in Kosovo calls for quick establishment of institutions so that the country continues with European integrations and required reforms. Meanwhile, a meeting of the chairperson of the session with the parliamentary group leaders was announced to be agreed for the next session where the constitution of the Kosovo parliament will be completed.

"The Kosovars are supporters of US policy in Europe and the global politics that run the US The Russian effort will fail in the Balkans. Russia has long lost this influence with the exception of keeping reports close to Serbia, while the latter in politics International has two chairs - one has the US and the EU and Russia on the other. But I say that the two-seat political game is the firstenough for the US and the EU. They want Serbia to have it in the EU, "says Blerim Burjani. But how far has Kosovo-US relations faded, the constant insistence of the President of Kosovo for transforming the KSF into a Kosovo army by law, because he is convinced that Kosovo Serb representatives will not vote on constitutional changes that would also enable the transformation of the KSF into the army? Analyst Blerim Burjani does not believe that this has shaken the US-Kosovo relations, because ultimately, according to him, the US will support Kosovo in every circumstance. "So the solution of our US friends should be proposed, how to establish a military. The US official has called for the establishment of the Armed Forces to happen gradually, step by step, and that opportunities should be established through the Constitution and the changes to take place So I understand his message to local institutions, and the other option can only come to an end if that fails, so I consider it sensible that Senator McCain's visit and US friends suggest, "says Blerim Burjani.

Big Coalitions

Political analysts, in turn, say a coalition involving a large number of political parties cannot be lasting. Blerim Burjani, the analyst says, "The NAP will form a non-life government and without any specific objective. It is a pity that the state will not be governed by law and order, but by anarchy and by many beneficiaries from all sides, "says Blerim Burjani.

EULEX
Another legal advisor, Blerim Burjani, tells DW that the Republic of Kosovo is still not consolidated to govern the rule and law at the level and standards of an independent and neutral justice, especially when it comes to political figures, or as they are known like 'big fish'. Kosovo needs a

justice reform that is indispensable for the state. EULEX is the product of this situation that reigns in Kosovo, where politicians have not always wanted to leave the functioning of justice independent. Kosovo is an independent state with transitional and lamentable justice. Kosovo's claim earlier was for the EULEX mission in Kosovo, while the Special Court is also unrelated to the unwillingness of Kosovo's institutions that immediately after the war should be established to disclose some cases that have been spoken by international diplomats. So Kosovo should have established such a court, and not expect the international community to do so, "says Blerim Burjani. Eksüperitz Burjani says that independent Kosovo with international missions such as EULEX or Special Court is indicating a fragility of the functioning of its legal system. "The paths of the EULEX mission are not in line with those of the Special Court, but there is a point in common because there was no strong will on the part of Kosovo's justice that to deal with such grave issues. The fate of justice in Kosovo unfortunately was related to the fate of politicians, so the policy was on justice and the consequences of justice and its organs, "Blerim Burjani says.Legal Issues Top criticism of the ineffectiveness of Kosovo's justice bodies is linked to the lack of political will in Kosovo to develop an independent justice system. That is why, according to them in Kosovo, international missions, such as EULEX and the Special Court, continue to be present, because Kosovo has not yet matured as a state to overcome its own challenge of the rule of law and the effective international standards and standards where the laws are implemented satisfactorily. The EULEX mission was established in Kosovo in November 2008 and now with the final decision of the Kosovo parliament this mission has a mandate until June 2018. While the Special Court decision, which will handle war crimes, is also ratified in Kosovo's parliament, but its functionality is expected this year.

Lunaqek in CEC

"PDK-AA-Nisma (PAN) does not have the majority to make the government, LDK-AKR-Alternative (LAA) does not enter into a coalition with the PAN or self-determination. to produce problems but not to solve the problems, or in this situation we should have a technical government or new elections if no one wants to go to PAN coalition, which means new elections again, "says Blerim Burjani.

Serbian List

Well-known politicians in Kosovo criticize the government for the approach they say are not serious about the establishment of the Armed Forces of Kosovo. Blerim Burjani, an analyst told DW, said that during the Kosovo-Serbia talks in Brussels, priority was given only to the Association Agreement of Serb-majority municipalities, leaving behind AFC.According to him, "the establishment of the Armed Forces of Kosovo (FAK) is indispensable to complement the establishment of Kosovo's state institutions."There is no reason to postpone or prevent the Serbian list. FAK will be a multiethnic armed force, which will be overseen by KFOR troops. FAK will work on the basis of its constitutional mandate and will respect the international presence and will be an additional mechanism for strengthening security in Kosovo together with KFOR. So far, there is an international consensus that FAK will be a militarily militarily equipped army in line with NATO standards and policies and the conditions and circumstances in the region, so it is expected to be an important factor in the defense of the state of Kosovo and peace in the region, "says Blerim Burjani.According to him, no one should be afraid of the Kosovo army, nor Serbia because, Kosovo is going to normalize relations with Serbia. Analyst Burjani recalls that earlier was neglected the case, that "by voting by the Special Court Assembly, in the package would be also the immediate vote of the Armed Forces of Kosovo".

Kosovo is rendered in crisis

Blerim Burjani, political analyst, told Deutsche Welle that "the political irresponsibility of politicians in Kosovo has surpassed every move". "The capture of one another, the position with the opposition, has led the way without a solution. This bizarre political and absurd stunt continues to plague the life of the citizen and democracy, both sides are thinking that they are good, I am saying that these political subjects in the country are in a critical state of the fierce struggle for power, or position or opposition.

Conditions not to go back, not the absolute interest to find solutions to the citizens, has overwhelmed the political scene with illegitimacy, have grossly politicized every pore of the life of the citizens, "says Blerim Burjani.However, despite calls to the opposition for dialogue, the leaders of the opposition parties do not seem to be shaken by their positions. They said that the agreements should be canceled and the MPs released, then they should be discussed. Five opposition MPs are in detention or under house arrest, while two others are in search of the police. All are accused of throwing tear gas in the Kosovo parliament. The opposition opposes the agreements for establishing a majority Serb-majority association and demarcation with Montenegro and for more than two months has blocked parliamentary sessions. The political crisis also led US Secretary of State John Kerry during his visit to Kosovo on (02.12) to appeal against the violence in parliament. He said that "the US would not support any agreement that would threaten Kosovo's sovereignty, security or independence".

Blerim Burjani, a connoisseur of political developments in Kosovo, told DW that the signing of recent agreements in Brussels is gradually completing the international strategic scenario for Kosovo."The Association of Serbian Municipalities was achieved as I have said several times that this association will have its own denomination, symbols, competencies of administration, education, health, social issues and economic development. While, constitutional changes are now expected. Within the Kosovo constitution, an association is established to secure this minority in Kosovo and the Armed Forces of Kosovo (FAK). Now, according to this scenario, the demarcation with Serbia and the recognition of Serbia from Kosovo can come as well. So it can be said that it can end an international strategic scenario, "says Blerim Burjani.However, opposition political parties and many civil society organizations have repeatedly accused the Kosovo government of not transparently negotiating and negotiating with Serbia. But this time, the Kosovo government decided to publish the agreement on the Association of Serb-majority municipalities in full, enabling everyone to read it in detail to defend their position as they say, "The Association of Wholesale Municipalities Burjani says it is better to go to extraordinary elections and to not block the work of the Kosovo Assembly. "Kosovo has to find another model of state governance, Kosovo has 76 political entities or 76 alternatives, so it is not an alternative to these four entities in the Assembly that are responsible for the state of affairs." The situation in Kosovo is quite sensitive, to chaos is the most unacceptable state in the state. Better extraordinary choices than the impasse of institutional life, "says Blerim Burjani.The Agreement for Association of Serb-majority Municipalities was reached on 25 August between Kosovo and Serbia, with the mediation of the European Union. The opposition sees it as a step that leads to the division of Kosovo. A day later on August 26, the agreement for demarcation between Kosovo and Montenegro was signed in Vienna. This agreement is also opposed by the opposition and the withdrawal of signature is required. Kosovo Prime Minister Isa Mustafa, who is on a visit to the United States, was not allowed to report to the Assembly for a couple of weeks before. He even shot eggs from opposition MPs. Prime Minister Isa Mustafa said that the agreements can not be returned to the zero point.

Special Court
Debate in parliament contradicts Kosovo's constitution
Well-known justice affair, Blerim Burjani, told DW that the parliamentary debate on court decisions contradicts Kosovo's constitution, which clearly defines the separation of power."In the internal aspect, it is harmed by justice and the resolution of cases independently and professionally no matter what the trial epilogue, this session is in contradiction with the values and principles that the constitution of the state makes, that the state believes In the constitutional democracy that emanates from the people and the state executive, the government is in touch with this topic. Injustice and justice are revealed through facts not through politics, "says Blerim Burjani. According to him, Kosovo is not part of the Council of Europe and for this fact if the policy claims that there is a human rights violation as it claims "in the case of former KLA commanders" then it can make the request for monitoring of trials by international human rights organizations. The special court, which will judge the possible crimes committed by former KLA members, is now at the conclusion of its staff consolidation. The special court seat has already been deployed in the Netherlands and its potential prisoners will also be extradited to Kosovo outside the EU in various places. Coalitions PDK and LDK

Blerim Burjani, from the Kosovo Institute for Development Policy (IKPZH), told DW that the coalition between the Democratic Party of Kosovo and the Democratic League of Kosovo (PDK-LDK) creates institutional sustainability."It is welcome to the international community, it favors international politics and its aims around the Balkan region. Kosovo will pass through this time period at several stages: the establishment of a special court, the implementation of the agreement for the north, prosecutions, expected to begin in March next year by EULX, the dialogue with Serbia to a neighborhood agreement good, constitutional changes in Kosovo etc ", says Blerim Burjani.

Violence is condemned in the Kosovo parliament :Meanwhile, political analysts say the political situation in Kosovo is not sustainable and according to them there are only two opportunities to get out of this crisis. Analyst Blerim Burjani told DW: "The position must be agreed with the opposition, so that it cannot continue with the blockade of the assembly or it should accept the blockade and the country should go to the polls. So how is it gone is lost sense and reason that of assembly because they are blocking the bulletin, "says Blerim Burjani.However, it is still unknown how the hearings will be held in the Kosovo parliament. Parliament Speaker Kadri Veseli says this blockade will not be allowed in infinity. The Prime Minister of Kosovo, Isa Mustafa, during a government meeting held the day before said that the processes in Kosovo can not be returned forwards, recalling once again that it does not intend to withdraw the signing from the agreement with Serbia for the establishment of the association of Serb majority municipalities.The institutional crisis in Kosovo is artificial, but not constitutional.Political analysts, on their part, for the delays in the creation of Kosovo institutions, are responsible for Kosovo's leadership, and not as stated earlier, the uncertainty surrounding the Kosovo Constitution. That was what Burjani, the Kosovo Institute for Development Policy (IEPP), told. "Exclusive or special responsibility falls on leadership. Aptitude for power, regardless of election result or electoral power reached by political parties in the last June 8th elections, and regardless of the two very clear verdicts of the Constitutional Court, it was expected to be over 5 months to ascertain these political subjects that they have no other way than to enforce the decisions of the Constitutional Court. These things have ruined the image of the country before the international community. The fierce struggle for power, which has surpassed all the democratic parameters for a new state, such as Kosovo, has greatly aggravated the lives of citizens, says Blerim Burjani.According to him, the citizens are tired of this leadership and feel bored and very depressed with the social, economic state that reigns within the state and without any perspectives that can be seen on the horizon."Then most of the political entities have big trouble with the rule of law, a large number of political entities inside them have people who are investigated by EULEX for unlawful acts, some of these cases are expected to go to the Special Court and these things have probably affected even more the non-establishment of central institutions. The constitution was clear there was no vacuum, which had adversely affected the constitution of central institutions, but the subjective interpretations made by political entities and some other individuals had caused confusion in this direction, "says Blerim Burjani. However, he thinks that in the foreseeable future the Constitution of Kosovo should be revisited to further reform this highest legal-political act of the state.It is still unknown when the continuation of the assembly session will be held It is still unclear, however, when the continuation of the constitutive session of the Kosovo Assembly will be held, where will be elected the Speaker of Parliament and the Presidency to open the way for the creation of the new government, although for the latter it is not yet known who can create the government. Officials of the Democratic Party of Kosovo continue to insist, requiring a comprehensive preliminary agreement between the political parties, in order to convene constitutive sessions and establish institutions. The international presence in Kosovo is constantly calling for the establishment of institutions, although so far has refused to interfere directly with Kosovar political subjects. Kosovo's image is damaged.Analyst Blerim Burjan says it does not matter how the work has come up here, "but this court should start work, no matter whether there are any facts or not, the idea was to uncover cases during the Kosovo war in 1999 from Dick Marty's report. " According to him, it would not be good for the case to be opened at the UN. "This would bring a great damage to Kosovo's image, so a part of UN history would remain in international drawers for cases judged in Kosovo, so it is better to conclude this issue in Kosovo without any noise or publicity international. " Electoral Reform :We have seen that political parties are not interested to have adequate legal reform for the elections, are not interested in Kosovo being divided into areas and to be the best citizen representation in the Kosovo Assembly. They are still comfortable in Kosovo to be just one electoral zone. This is especially appropriate for small parties, "says Blerim Burjani, who for several years has been a member of the CEC. Meanwhile, representatives of the Serb community in the electoral reform seek to include a point related to the continued mandate reserved for minorities. However, according to the Kosovo Constitution after the end of international supervision of independence, from the upcoming parliamentary elections, reserved seats become guaranteed seats. This means that minorities from the upcoming elections will not be able to take up to 20 seats in the Assembly from the beginning, plus the seats they can win by votes, but in total they can have only 20 seats guaranteed. 10 seats for the Serb community and 10 others for other minority communities.

Raising Salaries by Prime Minister Ramush Haradinaj

For his part, analyst Blerim Burjani agrees that the decision to increase salaries for the prime minister and his subordinates is defined by the anti-corruption law as a conflict of interest. According to him, if the broad legal basis in force of the state of Kosovo is interpreted is unlawful, the Kosovo Assembly should issue a law on salaries and salaries in the civil service. "It is not the only Prime Minister who has increased salaries for himself and his subordinates but are also the Pension Trust, the boards, the independent constitutional commissions, so even such budget institutions that raise their own salaries, even when these boards have allocated additional funds to members of the boards in some cases. Suspension of the Prime Minister's decision is the result of bringing the Constitutional Court to the decision on the unlawful raising of wages, so in such situations the decision until a Constitutional Court decision is suspended, "Burjani said, adding that any conflict of interest should be stopped, otherwise AKM has the right to file the case also to the state prosecutor's office. Burjani stressed that any decision should be balanced and legitimate. "Such a decision of the Prime Minister has faced in large opposition citizens and public opinion as an undetermined decision and detrimental to the citizens and the state budget, so each decision should be balanced and lawful. Competencies are clear, the Assembly should issue the law on salaries and leveling as soon as possible, to stop the anarchy and the will of the one party that numerous budget organizations increase their salaries without any decision of the sovereign, ie the Assembly representing the interests of citizens, "Burjani concluded.

Who won and who louse   in the national elections of June 2017

This is how political analyst Blerim Burjani thinks that Kosovo has no bigger party, according to him there is a confusion among citizens."From the two choices made at the national level, LVV has emerged from a winning party while the PDK has declined on both levels, while there was little increase in local elections AAK and LDK, there is no big party in Kosovo, there is a limit on the citizens, this was seen in two choices, in the national elections the citizens voted differently, but not that it was a positive vote for VV, rather it is a return to complete confusion, "Burjani said.According to him, in terms of positions and number of ministries, the biggest beneficiary in national elections was the Behxhet Pacolli.

The International Institute for Middle-East and Balkan Studies (**IFIMES**) **Following the initiative taken by Kosovo's and Serbia's Presidents to redraft the borders and in view of the alleged conclusion of the Belgrade-Pristina dialogue under the auspices of the European Union, IFIMES has prepared an analysis of the current political situation and its repercussions on the region and the international community it seems to give a fit back in the political relation. The most relevant and interesting sections from the comprehensive analysis entitled** "Kosovo-Serbia relations in 2018: The Vučić-Thaçi agreement for two million new refugees?" **are published below. President Thaci does not intend any change in the margins of this analysis, which seems to be an analytical product with a media title, but reality says something else, Presidium Thaci realistically requires only the union of three Albanian municipalities in Serbia to correct the borders of Kosovo and Serbia since 1956 no less than or no further, so this research**

has a more prophetic and realistic story of politics. This three municipal in Serbia Preseva,Bujanovci dhe Medvegja should belon to Kosovo as belong before 1956.

1. The Kosovo-Serbia dialogue with a clear goal

The proclamation of Kosovo's independence in 2008 intensified the problems between the newly formed Republic of Kosovo and the Republic of Serbia. Therefore, in 2011, the international community launched the dialogue between Belgrade and Priština under the auspices of the European Union. So far the dialogue has shown only modest results due to obstructions caused by the participating parties in their attempts to achieve certain goals. The prolongation of the dialogue has enabled political survival to certain politicians. That is why the deadline has been set to end the dialogue and reach the legally binding agreement between Serbia and Kosovo in the first half of 2019. The problem occurred when the Brussels dialogue provided for the formation of the Community of Serb Municipalities (ZSO) in northern Kosovo which is mostly populated by majority Serbian population. The Kosovo Constitutional Court decided that the proposed Statute on the formation of the Community of Serb Municipalities is contrary to certain provisions of the Kosovo Constitution. Besides the disputable provisions in the Statute there was a very strong political opposition against the formation of ZSO expressed by certain political parties, notably the Self-Determination movement (*Lëvizja Vetëvendosje* – LVV), which estimated that the formation of ZSO would cause irreparable damage to the statehood of the Republic of Kosovo as it would represent a kind of an entity within the state of Kosovo closely resembling the Republika Srpska entity within Bosnia and Herzegovina. After some other political parties also pointed to that risk, the project of forming ZSO was halted. However, the official Belgrade insists on the formation of ZSO which it believes to be crucial for the preservation of the Serbian community in Kosovo. This is only partly true, since ZSO would include about one third of all Serbs in Kosovo, while the remaining two thirds would still live in other parts of Kosovo. ZSO would be institutionally connected with the Belgrade authorities. This creates a model of special and parallel connections between ZSO and Serbia, similar to those between Serbia and the Republika Srpska entity in Bosnia and Herzegovina. In the meanwhile, the special war crimes court has started to try crimes allegedly committed by the Kosovo Liberation Army (UÇK). Its task is to prosecute some key Albanian politicians in Kosovo, including Kosovo President **Hashim Thaci**, Kosovo's Parliament *Speaker* **Kadri Veseli**, possibly also Prime Minister **Ramush Haradinaj** and many other high officials. The special court represents a kind of a mono-ethnic court since it was established to try only Albanians, which is a legal nonsense. Kosovo political leaders took the initiative to abolish the special court, but it was withdrawn under strong international pressures. It is through the Brussels dialogue that the Kosovo political leaders are actually trying to postpone the operation of the special court. The ultimate goal of the Brussels dialogue between Belgrade and Priština was to normalise the relations between the two states and reach mutual recognition, which would enable Serbia to accelerate its EU membership process and gain numerous financial benefits, while for Kosovo it would open the door to UN membership. Nevertheless, there are some other obstacles that may be encountered on Kosovo's road to UN membership, such as the veto imposed by UN permanent members – the Russian Federation and the People's Republic of China. Since Kosovo has still not been recognised by two thirds of UN member states, it can not gain the support for membership from the UN General Assembly.Under the present circumstances, Serbia – being a self-proclaimed neutral state – is carrying out intensive armament, while the Kosovo Government only enjoys minority support in the Parliament and Kosovo President Hashim Thaçi lacks public support. Analysts believe that the solution for the present situation would be to carry out an early election in Kosovo, which would show the real relations between political forces in this country. **A**fter **Aleksandar Vučić** and Hashim Thaçi, by arbitrary action, took over the dialogue which should be led by prime ministers of Serbia and Kosovo, they took the initiative to correct and redefine state borders, which in their own language represents the historical borderline between the Serbs and Albanians. Vučić and Thaçi suspended the constitutional role of prime ministers, stole the state institutions and unconstitutionally established the presidential system in their countries. They received support from certain states for their borderline initiative, according to which the two countries would exchange territories and inhabitants so that the northern Kosovo would belong to Serbia (thus it would no longer be necessary to form ZSO), while most of the Preševo valley (Preševo, Medvedja and Bujanovac – regarded as"east Kosovo") would belong to Kosovo (to which it had actually belonged till 1956). The realisation of such an agreement would lead to massive resettlement of inhabitants and the formation of ethnic borders. According to Vučić and Thaçi this would solve the problem by enabling permanent demarcation of borders between Serbs and Albanians. However, analysts warn that this would not solve the problem but instead cause new conflicts, victims, tragedies and at least two million new refugees. Another figure involved in this initiative is Albanian Prime Minister **Edi Rama.** He is surrounded by advisers from Kosovo who had strong connections with Milošević regime in 1990s – just like Vučić and Dačić, who now symbolise that regime. Kosovo opposition strongly rejects the borderline initiative, demanding President Thaçi to abandon the idea that may have devastating repercussions for Kosovo and calling for an emergency meeting of the Parliament to discuss the issue. Even Kosovo Prime Minister Ramush Haradinaj opposed the initiative, stating that *"Any change to the borders and exchange of the territories will trigger new tragedies in the Balkans and may lead to instability and undermine long-term political and security efforts for peace in Kosovo and the region"*. Although all previous wars in the territory of SFRY were fought in order to change the borders, those borders were never changed. The wars only brought new problems. The question is whether this would be the right way to resolve problems for the countries whose ambition is to gain EU membership. The EU is based on diversity, and many EU states are multiethnic, multicultural and multi-confessional, which makes the Vučić-Thaçi initiative anti-civilizational and anti-European. However, the initiative veils Vučić's attempts to save at least some of the failed Greater Serbia project designed by **Slobodan Milošević**. Aleksandar Vučić and **Ivica Dačić** actually symbolise Milošević's politics from 1990s, and according to that plan the loss of a part of the territory in Kosovo would be compensated by annexation of a part of the territory of Bosnia and Herzegovina, i.e. Republika Srpska. The Greater Serbia project even includes parts of Montenegro and Croatia. Pro-Serbian political parties in Montenegro which are members of the Democratic Front (DF) opposition have together with the Serbian national council already started to create the atmosphere by launching the activities for gathering the signatures for the petition to annul Montenegro's decision to recognize Kosovo's independence. The realization of the Vučić-Thaçi agreement would cause tectonic changes in the region, leading to new conflicts, victims, tragedies and a new wave of at least two million refugees who would have to seek shelter in EU states, notably Germany and Austria. Therefore, those who support such an agreement will have to take responsibility for its consequences. Nevertheless, Macedonia is of an even greater importance for Vučić's project at the moment. Since Aleksandar (Vučić) arrived too late to Kosovo[1] to resolve the Kosovo issue, he will have to redirect his activities to Macedonia.Macedonia has always been a part of the Greater Serbia project. It is not surprising that Serbia only recognised Macedonia on 8 April 1996, that is after the wars ended and Milošević's Greater Serbia project collapsed.Notably, Serbian security and intelligence structures participated in the obstructions carried out during the formation of the new government of the Republic of Macedonia led by **Zoran Zaev** (SDSM), and the officials of the Serbian Security Information Agency (BIA) were involved in the incident in the Sobranie (Macedonian Parliament) when Zoran Zaev and some of his colleagues were attacked in an assassination attempt. Former *security* adviser at Serbia's *Embassy* in Skopje and BIA's deputy director **Goran Živaljević** was present in the Sobranie during the incident . The regime of **Nikola Gruevski** and **Saša Mijalkov** closely cooperated with the Belgrade regime. Moreover, numerous transactions and the pulling of money out of Macedonia were carried out through Serbia and with the assistance of Serbian authorities. Serbia was one of a few countries that did not support the Macedonia-Greece agreement which resolved the decades-long dispute about the constitutional name of Macedonia. The agreement with Greece was even supported by Russia and the controversial Hungarian Prime Minister **Viktor Orbán**, while Serbia's Foreign Minister Ivica Dačić announced that Serbia would withdraw its recognition of the Republic of Macedonia under its constitutional name. The meetings between Serbian and Macedonian governments have been called off several times, while bilateral meetings between high officials and ministers are a true rarity. Serbia appointed the controversial diplomat and former BIA director **Rade Bulatović** as its new ambassador to Macedonia. At the same time, Serbia has strengthened its (para)intelligence activities in Macedonia. The media controlled by Aleksandar Vučić constantly spread disinformation and lies about Macedonian Prime Minister Zoran Zaev and his closest co-workers.In only one year, the new government of the Republic of Macedonia consolidated the internal situation in the country and achieved significant foreign political results. A significant contribution to this achievements was made by Macedonia's Minister of Interior **Oliver Spasovski**, who managed to strengthen the country's security-intelligence system and its capacity to resist security-intelligence attacks from abroad. Serbia has increased the presence of its (para)intelligence apparatus in Macedonia in view of the referendum scheduled for 30 September 2018. Once the agreement with Greece is finally approved at the referendum, no one can stop Macedonia on its way to NATO and EU membership. Serbia disapproves Macedonia's accession to NATO, believing it would jeopardise its national interests. On the other hand, it allows open functioning of the Serbian-Russian Humanitarian Centre in Niš, which actually represents the first Russian military base in the territory of Serbia and thus a direct threat to Macedonia and Kosovo.Nevertheless, the key reason why Serbia has increased the presence of its (para)intelligence apparatus in Macedonia it to prevent the positive outcome of the referendum, since a successful referendum will be followed by the canonical recognition of Macedonian Orthodox Church. This year, theArchbishopric of Ohrid celebrates the 1000th anniversary of its founding. Since orthodox churches are national churches, Macedonian Orthodox Church will be recognised once the name of the country is confirmed at the referendum. Serbian authorities act in symbiosis with Serbian Orthodox Church, so it is obvious why they are trying to prevent canonical recognition of Macedonian Orthodox Church.

Perfidy of Vučić's politics towards Macedonia

While at first sight it may seem that Vučić's current activities are focused on Kosovo and Republika Srpska (Bosnia and Herzegovina), he harbours secret ambitions towards Macedonia. On 2 September 2018, Vučić met Macedonian Prime Minister Zaev at the Preševo -Tabanovce border crossing to announce the implementation of joint border management, while at the same time he carries out activities with the goal to disintegrate Macedonia. This clearly shows the perfidy of Vučić's politics towards Macedonia.Therefore it is of crucial importance to stop the Vučić-Thaçi initiative and their intentions to change the borders. At the special parliamentary session Kosovo Parliament is expected to adopt a resolution that would ban Kosovo President Hashim Thaci from further negotiating with Belgrade about changing the territory of Kosovo and resettling its inhabitants. The Assembly of the Republic of Kosovo is also expected to consider a motion of impeachment of President Thaçi due to his unconstitutional activities that are undermining Kosovo's territorial integrity. The best answer to Vučić's attempts will be given by Macedonian citizens who will support the referendum and confirm the agreement signed on 18 June 2018 between the Republic of Macedonia and the Republic of Greece. This will accelerate Macedonia's accession to NATO and EU and open the door to canonical recognition of Macedonian Orthodox Church and correction of historical injustice it has suffered. The Republic of Macedonia will thus consolidate its statehood and ensure a better future for all its citizens.

Ljubljana, 6 September

2018

[1] Translator's note: The saying "Too late Marko to Kosovo arrives" (Serbian: *Kasno Marko na Kosovo stiže*) stems from the national epic poem that mentions how Prince Marko, who was regarded as the Slavic national hero, arrived too late to Kosovo where the Ottoman Empire army had already won the battle. The saying is often used to denote an action or reaction that is too late.

German press

At least the optimists from Brussels have not lost their confidence yet. There are "realistic chances" that the presidents of Serbia and Kosovo could come to an agreement "to solve all open issues between Belgrade and Pristina", EU foreign policy chief Federica Mogherini hopefully announced before the continuation of the forced EU dialogue of the two controversial ex-war opponents this Friday in Brussels: "The next few months are crucial." The reluctant negotiating partners are struggling more and more nervously for the neighborhood agreement demanded by the EU until next spring. But despite the end-time sentiment, especially in Brussels and Belgrade, a speedy end to the tough Kosovo tug-of-war is not in sight. Because in Pristina resistance against Belgrade's favored territorial exchange is growing -and against President Hashim Thaci as a negotiator. Since 2008, Kosovo, which is now recognized by more than 110 UN states, is independent. But the state newcomer is still denied access to important international organizations because of the continuing barrage of Belgrade and Moscow. Conversely, there is an increasing pressure on EU candidate Serbia to actually recognize the long-lost Kosovo: The EU, which is already tired of enlargement,does not feel like importing bilateral problems. For a long time Belgrade was hardly heard with demands for a separation of the almost exclusively Serb-settled northern Kosovo in the west. Any border adjustment could trigger a dangerous chain reaction in the ex-Yugoslav multinational empire, according to the unanimous warning from politicians, diplomats and civil rights groups: changing the borders of Kosovo could undermine the secessionist desires of Serb and Croat minorities in Bosnia, but also those of the Macedonian Give new food to Albanians.Approval for "Border corrections":

But the US and EU are increasingly exhausted by the Kosovo permanent construction site. In addition, the mandate of the current EU Commission expires next year. In a kind of concerted action, US and EU diplomats have in recent weeks signaled their approval of the scenario of "demarcation" or "border adjustments", which was launched mainly by Vucic, but most recently also by Thaci, but has not yet been explained. But not only because Berlin and London continue to reject a change of borders, Brussels course change is problematic. In Serbia, too, a possible division of Kosovo meets with criticism - and in Pristina, both the government and the opposition are clearly opposed. With his own pathos, Vucic has announced "the most important speech" of his life for his Kosovo visit on Sunday, in order to convince the skeptical Kosovo Serbs of the need to balance Pristina. While Serbia's Dominator has the media power and political backing to crack his doubter compatriots' deal, Thaci is largely isolated in his own country with his push for frontier corrections for the incorporation of Serbia's Albanian Presevo Valley: even his PDK is skeptical about area exchanges.President Thaci does not have the authority to negotiate borders, Prime Minister Ramush Haradinaj is angry. But with the common intention to show the presidential soloist Thaci the borders in the border dispute, blocked in Kosovo's parliament, the governing and opposition parties each other. Instead of reaching an agreement, the Brussels Dialogue threatens to bring the state newcomer one of the worst crises in his ten-year history: even new elections are no longer ruled out in Pristina.The annual conference organized on Tuesday focused on strengthening economic cooperation between Albania, Bosnia-Herzegovina, Kosovo, Macedonia, Montenegro and Serbia. In addition, the expansion of the ailing infrastructure and the processing of the wars in the break-up of Yugoslavia (1991-1999) are central themes.A few hours before the start of the conference, a serious quarrel broke out between Serbia and its former province of Kosovo. Belgrade threatened after the arrest of five compatriots in Kosovo with the end of the EU-mediated Kosovo dialogue. "If the five detainees are not released by evening, there will be no dialogue in the long term," said the Serbian government for Kosovo Marko Djuric in Belgrade. "For me, this is cowardly, bestial and outrageous behavior," the politician continues. Kosovo law enforcement agencies have released a decompression sign by releasing the five Serbs in the afternoon after interrogation. Special forces of the Kosovo police had arrested the Serbs in the region of the municipality Gjilane southeast of the capital Pristina. They are said to have worked against the country's constitution, said parliamentary president Kadri Veseli.

The release of the Serbian ultimatum to end the dialogue has evidently averted a major setback in the West's decades of compromise efforts. Kosovo, which is almost exclusively inhabited by Albanians, has been independent of Serbia since 2008. Belgrade does not recognize this and wants to have its former province back.

Merkel wants a European perspective for the Balkans

Despite all objections to a rapid EU enlargement, German Chancellor Angela Merkel is counting on the further rapprochement of the Western Balkan states to Brussels. It was about "equipping the region with a European perspective," Merkel said after the conference.

With this aim, the connection between these countries should be strengthened. This could be done through the expansion of infrastructure, economic cooperation and a broad youth exchange. (Nag / SDA)

Created: 10.07.2018,

European Commission - Press release

Commission opens dialogue with Kosovo on visa-free entry Brussels, 19 January 2012 - EU Commissioner for Home Affairs Cecilia Malmström has opened today in Pristina the dialogue on visa liberalization with Kosovo. The aim is to lift the visa requirement for citizens of Kosovo, provided that their government undertakes fundamental reforms, i.a. successfully implemented in the following key areas: forgery of travel documents, border management, migration and asylum control, public security and order (in particular the fight against organized crime and corruption) and fundamental rights issues related to the free movement of persons.
"We have the firm intention to abolish the visa requirement for Kosovo and can now start to implement it. I know how important it is for citizens of Kosovo to travel without a visa, and I am pleased that the first step has now been taken. However, whether and how quickly we achieve our goal depends solely on the Kosovar government continuing its rule of law reform efforts, with concrete progress being made, "said Cecilia Malmström.In the past, the EU had already engaged in dialogue with five Western Balkan countries on the liberalization of visa requirements in order to allow their

citizens visa-free entry into the EU. Following an assessment of progress in the implementation of key reforms, the visa requirement for the former Yugoslav Republic of Macedonia, Montenegro and Serbia (IP / 09/1852) was lifted in December 2009, followed in November 2010 by Albania and Bosnia and Herzegovina (MEMO / 10 / 548).

Background

Bilateral meetings were held today between Commissioner Malmström and Prime Minister Hashim Thaçi,
 During her visit to Kosovo (19-20 January), Commissioner Malmström will also meet with the EU's Rule of Law Mission (EULEX), Xavier Bout de Marnhac, as well as with non-governmental organizations, think tanks and academia.In Pristina she will visit the Center for Victims and the fight against trafficking. This is a non-profit organization providing social and legal assistance to victims and potential victims of trafficking, providing temporary secure housing and education and training opportunities. In addition, Commissioner Malmström will visit the Selman Riza School in Fushë Kosovë / Kosovo Polje, which recently welcomed 42 children from different communities (Roma, Ashkali and Egyptians) who had not attended school for several years. Police operation: Serbian list withdraws from Kosovo governmentAfter the short-term arrest of Serbian politician Marko Đurić, the Serbian list wants to found the municipality without Prishtina Adelheid Wölfl

March 27, 2018, 19:45

Marko Đurić is arrested

APA / AFP

On Tuesday, the Serbian list - the most important Serbian party in the Kosovar government - announced its withdrawal from the cabinet. The break with the Kosovar government went quickly. Secondly, the leadership of the Serbian list announced that it would create the Serbian community association itself, without the help of Prishtina. The Serbian Association of

Municipalities was decided in 2013, but never implemented. But just on Monday, when Marko Đurić, the Serbian director for Kosovo, came to Kosovo, the implementation should start from the Kosovar side. But then Đurić was arrested.

Back in Serbia he appeared with bandage around the wrists at the press conference. The picture message caused emotional ups and downs in Serbia. Marko Đurić also told terrible stories. So he had been threatened by a Kosovar police officer with a knife, another policeman had him a Kalashnikov held against his stomach. At the time of the arrest, the police called "Allahu Akbar". He was pulled like a dog and tried to humiliate him and the Serbian nation. He said he was proud of the self-defense of the Serbs following Gandhi's method.
Visit not allowed.

What happened? Đurić wanted to visit the North Kosovar city of Mitrovica on Monday to hold talks with citizens about the so-called internal dialogue on the future of Kosovo. He informed the Kosovar Government about his visit, as required by the regulations. However, the Kosovar government rejected the visit and did not allow it. Incidentally, this has already happened more often - even from the other side. The former Kosovar President Atifete Jahjaga was denied entry into Serbia around 2017. A video of a Serbian journalist shows the police operation. RTS Sajt - Zvanični canal.
But ćurić announced that he wanted to enter anyway. The Kosovar government announced that it would arrest illegal immigrants - as the law requires. But ćurić came to Mitrovica. Then he was arrested there by the special unit, led to Prishtina and brought back to the border with Serbia after completing the formalities. Some Kosovo Serbs were reportedly injured in North Mitrovica as part of the arrest because they tried to prevent them.
President Aleksandar Vucic called an immediate meeting of the National Security Council and telephoned Russian President Vladimir Putin, which he represented as a protecting power. He said that the starting points for the dialogue with Kosovo are now "different". "Terrorists" kidnapped Đurić, he said, "maybe because Marko did not recognize their terrorist state," he said. Vučić also criticized the EU mission Eulex. Because the special units of the Kosovar police, who arrested Đurić, were accompanied by vehicles of the Eulex. This combination of police and Eulex is common in northern Kosovo.

"The Albanian terrorists wanted to show the power that they have and the support of the West, and I thank them for this information," said Vučić, completely in the role of victim. However, he himself had refused to telephone with Western diplomats.

Serbian tentative: To "Occupy the north of Kosovo"

Finally, according to the Serbian website B92, the president said that the question of why Serbs were harassed was not answered by the EULEX. "It's their job to occupy the north of Kosovo," he said, obviously sarcastically. But "neither the Albanian nor their Western partners could harm citizens in northern Kosovo, because Serbia will not allow the safety of its citizens to be endangered" declared by nationalist politic of Serbia .

Also Đurić brought after the incident on Monday the territorial issue into play. He said the actions of the Kosovar police would be an attempt to "take possession" of the Serb-inhabited northern part of Kosovo. The same was said by the President of the Serbian List, Goran Rakić. It is also possible to interpret the statements of the two politicians in such a way that even during the action they wanted to signal that Northern Kosovo should remain with Serbia in the future.
Dialog questioned
EU foreign policy chief Federica Mogherini immediately went to Belgrade, but the dialogue has been very slow and sluggish for a long time. Đurić even indirectly denied further dialogue with Prishtina: "I think both sides have shown with their actions what they think about dialogue," he said. And Vučić.

Conclusions

- Talks on the final status of Kosovo in Austria, Kosovo declared independence in accordance with agreement in international community, Kosovo has become an independent state supported by the will of the people of Kosovo.

- The Ahtisaari plan is based on a well analysis , which plan secure minorities and offer to them privileged political and juridical status as minority living in state of Kosovo.
- Over a period of time has been mentioned by Serbia the political project for Ahtisaari plus solution, therefore new solutions for solutions, but so far it has not been made public that there is such a document, which according to the state of Kosovo is unacceptable.
- So far there have been little public debates in the Kosovo on this topic that there may be another document besides Ahtisaari for a consistent solution from Serbia in the near future.
- The so-called dialogue was not transparent for the citizens of both states Kosovo and Serbia.
- Agreements made in Brussels between the two countries have been implemented very little.
- Serbia has not respected any agreement while Kosovo has been stuck in implementing the agreement for the Association of Serbian Municipalities in Kosovo.
- Association of Serbian Municipalities should be a voluntary consultation mechanism of municipalities, so joining in this association should be non-mandatory.
- Dialogue Kosovo-Serbia may take another step if the parties agree, unless the Ahtisaari plan in force remains in force.
- The opening of any new political chapter besides the technical one approved by the UN would be a threat to the Balkan region that is full of such ethnic troubles. Pandora boxing means anarchy and not stability in the Balkans, this is what Russia wants.
- Technical Corrigendum and the Kosovo Border Marking - 1974 is the only acceptable regional and inter-communitarian border, any territorial exchange or correction to make new borders is dangerous for the region and for Europe.
- Kosovo and Serbia should conclude a final agreement on the eminence and respect of the borders and at least a firm agreement to respect the existing borders of 1974. States should establish a border between two neighboring states and within a reasonable

period of time must be legalized an international boundary between the two countries Kosovo and Serbia.

- In the final Kosovo document -Serbia, the issue of Albanians in Presheva, Bujanovci and Medvegja should be treated for a higher degree of political and civil liberties.
- Kosovo and Serbia should build peace relations in the region and respect their neighbors.
- The two countries should have good relations and integrate into the European Union, which is the goal of the state of Kosovo and the state of Serbia, to be part of the European Union.
- Literature:

1. Constitution of the Republic of Kosovo

2. Agency of statistics of the Republic of Kosovo

3.Blerim Burjani, Interpretation of Law, 2011, Prishtina

4.Institute for Development Policy (IKPZH)

5.News Paper interview

6.Blerim Burjani interview for Douche Welle

7.Blerim Burjani interview for Radio Free Europe

8.Kosovo-UNDP,Antiuccuptions , http: //www.undp. org/content/dam/kosovo/img/demgov/ SAEK/2013.04. 29%20SAEK%20Project%20Document%20for%20SDC-K.pdf

9.Ministry of Foreign Affairs of the Republic of Kosovo

10..Blerim Burjani, International Crises 2010 , Pristina

8.Blerim Burjani, Electoral Reform 2014

9.Newspaper: Kosovo Sot 2014

10.Alice Lacourt , Ralph Wilde , Kosovo: International Law and Recognition

11.New York Times

12. Newspaper: The Voice

13.Radio Free Europe

14.EU –Kosovo
https://eeas.europa.eu/delegations/kosovo/1387/node/1387_en,18.01.201
Pulsi Publik, UNDP, 2017
Blerim Burjani, Huumtim per gjedjen e te drejtave te njeriut ne Kosove,
Instituti i Kosoves per Politika Zhvillimore,2014

Data for Author:
Blerim Burjani was born in Pristina, in capital city of state of Kosovo. Primary and secondary school finish at his birthplace. Law Faculty in the University of Pristina general direction . Magistrates studies at the Law Faculty of the University of Pristina. Until now hold a series of public functions such is Political Adviser to the Minister of Labour and Social Welfare, Political Advisor in the Ministry of Trade and Industry, Representatives of the Government of Kosovo in CEFTA, the former member of the CEC. Blerim has experienc 15 years in high education as a lecturor professor at the Business College, was a professor in the College and University of Pristina ,College Dardania FAMA. In public opinion is known as an expert in development policies and political analyst and executive director of the Kosovo Institute for Development Policy. He has worked for a range of local and international organizations as follows: Council of Europe, KIPA, Human Dynamic in Vienna (Austria), B & S Strategy in Europe, World Bank, UNDP,USAID/RIINVEST, ECMI. He speaks and writes in two international languages: English and Spanish. He lives in Pristina. Books published by author:
Free press and democratization of society
Concept for Kosovo foreign policy
Interpretation of Law
Right or Left Political Parties Orientations in Western Balkan: Rights and Left Stats in Balkan ect.

I want morebooks!

Buy your books fast and straightforward online - at one of world's fastest growing online book stores! Environmentally sound due to Print-on-Demand technologies.

Buy your books online at
www.morebooks.shop

Kaufen Sie Ihre Bücher schnell und unkompliziert online – auf einer der am schnellsten wachsenden Buchhandelsplattformen weltweit! Dank Print-On-Demand umwelt- und ressourcenschonend produziert.

Bücher schneller online kaufen
www.morebooks.shop

Printed by Books on Demand GmbH, Norderstedt / Germany